COLLABORATIONS & CONFLICTS

A Leader Through Time

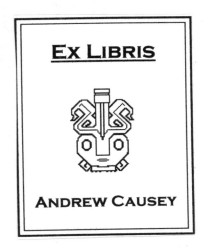

Ongka with conus shell nose decoration, 1971.

COLLABORATIONS & CONFLICTS
A Leader Through Time

ANDREW STRATHERN

and

PAMELA J. STEWART

HARCOURT COLLEGE PUBLISHERS

Fort Worth   Philadelphia   San Diego   New York   Orlando   Austin   San Antonio
Toronto   Montreal   London   Sydney   Tokyo

Publisher	Earl McPeek
Acquisitions Editor	Lin Marshall
Project Editor	Claudia Gravier
Art Director	Carol Kincaid
Production Manager	Andrea Archer

ISBN: 0-15-502147-8
Library of Congress Catalog Card Number: 99-62188

Address for Domestic Orders
Harcourt Inc., 6277 Sea Harbor Drive, Orlando, FL 32887-6777
800-782-4479

Address for International Orders
International Customer Service
Harcourt Inc., 6277 Sea Harbor Drive, Orlando, FL 32887-6777
407-345-3800
(fax) 407-345-4060
(e-mail) hbintl@harcourtbrace.com

Address for Editorial Correspondence
Harcourt College Publishers, 301 Commerce Street, Suite 3700,
Fort Worth, TX 76102

Web Site Address
http://www.harcourtcollege.com

Harcourt College Publishers will provide complimentary supplements or supplement packages to those adopters qualified under our adoption policy. Please contact your sales representative to learn how you qualify. If as an adopter or potential user you receive supplements you do not need, please return them to your sales representative or send them to: Attn: Returns Department, Troy Warehouse, 465 South Lincoln Drive, Troy, MO 63379.

Printed in the United States of America

9 0 1 2 3 4 5 6 7 8 751 9 8 7 6 5 4 3 2 1

Harcourt College Publishers

ABOUT THE SERIES

These case studies in cultural anthropology are designed for students in beginning and intermediate courses in the social sciences, to bring them insights into the richness and complexity of human life as it is lived in different places. The authors are men and women who have lived in the societies they write about and who are professionally trained as observers and interpreters of human behavior. Also, the authors are teachers; in their writing, the needs of the student reader remain foremost. It is our belief that when an understanding of ways of life very different from one's own is gained, abstractions and generalizations about the human condition become meaningful.

The scope and character of the series has changed constantly since we published the first case studies in 1960, in keeping with our intention to represent anthropology as it is. We are concerned with the ways in which human groups and communities are coping with the massive changes wrought in their physical and sociopolitical environments in recent decades. We are also concerned with the ways in which established cultures have solved life's problems. And we want to include representation of the various modes of communication and emphasis that are being formed and reformed as anthropology itself changes.

We think of this series as an instructional series, intended for use in the classroom. We, the editors, have always used case studies in our teaching, whether for beginning students or advanced graduate students. We start with case studies, whether from our own series or from elsewhere, and weave our way into theory, and then turn again to cases. For us, they are the grounding of our discipline.

ABOUT THE AUTHORS

Professor Andrew Strathern and Dr. Pamela J. Stewart (Strathern) are a husband and wife team working in the Hagen, Pangia, and Duna areas of the Highlands of Papua New Guinea. They also conduct research in the Lowlands of Scotland.

Andrew Strathern was born the fourth of five children in the small village of Birch near Colchester in England. His family originates from Ayrshire in Scotland, and most of his relatives are farming people. He was educated at the Colchester Royal Grammar School and at Trinity College Cambridge, where he studied classics and social anthropology. He has carried out long-term fieldwork in three different areas of the Papua New Guinea Highlands (Hagen, Pangia, Duna) since 1964, and has held academic posts in Cambridge, Canberra, Port Moresby, London (where he was Professor of Anthropology 1976–83), and Pittsburgh, where he has been A.W. Mellon Professor of Anthropology since 1987. He was awarded the Royal Anthropological Institute's Curl Essay Prize in 1968, the Rivers Memorial medal for field work in 1976, and the Papua New Guinea Tenth Anniversary of Independence medal in 1987.

He has pursued a very broad range of interests within anthropology, including kinship theory, exchange, ritual, social change and history, politics and violence, embodiment theory, and medical anthropology, and has published extensively on these and other topics, e.g. *Body Thoughts* (1996), and *Bodies and Persons* (co-edited with Michael Lambek 1998).

Pamela J. Stewart (Strathern) works with her husband, Andrew Strathern, as his collaborator and colleague in their jointly conducted fieldwork in Papua New Guinea and Scotland and through their archival research projects and creative writing. She has had the great fortune to travel, live, and work in many parts of the world where she has experienced global cultural diversity first-hand.

Drs. Stewart and Strathern are co-editors of the Journal of Ritual Studies and are Editor and Associate Editor of the Association for Social Anthropology in Oceania's Monograph Series, published by the University of Pittsburgh Press. They have collaborated on the latest revision of Roger Keesing's *Cultural Anthropology,* published by Harcourt Brace in 1998. They have recently co-edited *Millennial Markers* (1997) and *Kuk Heritage: Issues and Debates in Papua New Guinea* (1998), and co-authored *Curing and Healing: Medical Anthropology in Global Perspective* (1999). Besides a continuing program of research on Papua New Guinea they are engaged in a comparative project on Eastern Indonesian and Melanesian ethnographies and in ongoing research work on farming families and senses of identity in Lowland Scotland.

Ongka and Andrew Strathern

Ongka and Pamela J. Stewart

ABOUT THIS CASE STUDY

This life story of Ongka, a leader among the Kawelka people of Mount Hagen, Papua New Guinea is a most welcome addition to the offerings of the case studies in Cultural Anthropology. The series has always been especially open to biographies and autobiographies. Morris Opler's *Apache Odyssey,* was the first published followed over the years by Ruth Underhill's *Papago Woman,* David Jones's *Comanche Medicine Woman,* and most recently by Roger Keesing's *Elota's Story: The Life and Times of a Solomon Islands Big Man,* and with Ongka's life story we are publishing *Maori Woman,* by Mark K. Duffie.

Life stories in whatever form add a dimension to one's understanding of a culture different than one's own by bringing the person into the scene. Too often ethnographic descriptions are too generalized and the individual drops out. The reader has no one to identify with or compare with one's self. With the life story spread out before one's eyes, not only the individual person but the inside of the culture is revealed in an intimate, close-up way. We learn about Ongka as a leader, a man active in the affairs of his community, not only active, but in a commanding role. Though the specific contexts in which his leadership is occurring are different than our own, his motivations seem somehow clear to us.

His mixture of self-interest in the welfare of others is something we might well experience. His moments of anger and irritation, his pleasures, the self-congratulatory moments of despair and depression, all seem very human and therefore understandable, despite the "otherness" of the culture in which he is operating.

Tracing his life through time, from before the arrival of outsiders, particularly whites, through the years up to the present, chronicles immense and dramatic changes that have taken place in the Mt. Hagen area and in the New Guinea Highlands. These changes parallel those that have taken place in other vast areas of the contemporary world as the traditional way of life has been turned upside down and new, alien ways have become dominant.

Seeing these changes through Ongka's eyes gives us direct access, unfiltered by the ethnographers. The authors have kept their interventions discreetly submerged. One has the sense that Ongka is truly telling his own story.

I highly recommend this new case study for your reading and pleasure. And when I say pleasure I mean that it is a good read, captivating and exciting, as well as informative.

George Spindler, Editor
Case Studies in Cultural Anthropology

Preface

The genesis of the main part of this book, Ongka's life story, occurred in 1975, in Port Moresby, the capital city of Papua New Guinea, where the book's central character and narrator, Ongka, a leader among the Kawelka people of Mount Hagen, had been invited by the University of Papua New Guinea for the first showing there of the film *Ongka's Big Moka* (made for the Disappearing World series by Granada Television; directed by Charlie Nairn). The film was about Ongka's struggles to stage a huge ceremonial gift of pigs to his allies among the Tipuka tribe. Ongka was pleased to be invited but felt there was more to say beyond the film itself. And so his life history was recorded.

Ongka sat down in the prehistory laboratory in the Anthropology and Sociology department of the University, where he was surrounded by stone axes, clay pots, and wooden tools from Papua New Guinea's past, and began to give his story, which was recorded on a small cassette tape recorder. He became fully engrossed, gesturing and smiling into the microphone. The result was this narrative, translated and slightly rearranged to suit the form of a book. A few passages were omitted, and a few linking sentences were added. Parenthetical endnotes have been supplied in places where background information was needed; all other notes are details provided by Ongka himself. Some personal names and passages that Ongka included have been omitted for the sake of privacy.

It has been a pleasure to work over these materials again and to reflect further on Ongka's words and the sharp, inventive, accurately observed, and uncompromisingly straightforward portraits he gives of his society. Ongka describes an intricate network of friends and enemies, wars and exchanges, links between ecological zones, memories, and comparisons of past and future. Particularly striking and poignant are his concerns for his country at the time of its independence in 1975. Much has been achieved in Papua New Guinea since then, but many problems have emerged, some of them along the lines that Ongka predicted.

We wish to thank Harcourt College Publishers for agreeing to take on this project: Lin Marshall, Acquisitions Editor; Claudia Gravier, Project Editor; Carol Kincaid, Art Director; and Andrea Archer, Production Manager. Also thanks to Ms. Lee Tarullo for retyping the bulk of the original text and Mr. Craig Seder of the University of Pittsburgh's Cathedral Publishing for scanning the remainder, and Ongka himself for his inimitable and challenging presence among the Kawelka people throughout his adult life. We thank also the James Cook University of North Queensland for providing us with office space for the Centre for Pacific Studies, in which the introduction to the book was composed in 1998.

Contents

Preface   ix
List of Illustrations   xiii
Chronology   xv
Introduction   xvii

Chapter 1   A Thunderclap Gone Mad   1

Chapter 2   Games and Tricks   11

Chapter 3   Where Are You, Boys?   19

Chapter 4   My First Wife   25

Chapter 5   Special Foods   37

Chapter 6   War   41

Chapter 7   Attracting Wealth   51

Chapter 8   The Firethong Test   57

Chapter 9   Driving Out Warfare   63

Chapter 10   My Personal Enemies   67

Chapter 11   Wind Work   75

Chapter 12   The Jimi Valley   79

Chapter 13   Moka   91

Chapter 14   White Men Come and Go   111

Chapter 15   Songs   119

Chapter 16   Yara Speaks   131

Indexes   141

List of Illustrations

Page ii   Ongka decorated for a dance in November 1971. His conus-shell decoration and Local Government Councillor's badge are prominent.

Page vi   Ongka and Andrew J. Strathern.

Page vii   Ongka and Pamela J. Stewart.

Page 9   Ongka as a Local Government Councillor in 1970 (picture by Sandy Lawson).

Page 31   Ongka's wife Rumbukl and her daughter Yara decorated for a dance in November 1971.

Page 32   Yara and companion at the dance, November 1971.

Page 33   Rumbukl at the dance, held at Maninge ceremonial ground. She is a leader in the women's dancing and here takes a brief rest.

Page 34   Rumbukl and companion lead a group of female dancers, beating hour-glass drums.

Page 35   Ongka's son by Rumbukl, Namba (in centre) dances with other schoolboys at a celebration for Papua New Guinea's Self-Government (prior to Independence in 1975). The boys are holding the country's national flag, and Namba has borrowed Ongka's gold-colored chain.

Page 83   1975. At his old settlement place at Mbukl, Ongka makes an invocation to spirits of his own sub-clan in pairs, calling to them to ensure his continuing good luck in exchange, hunting (especially in the Jimi Valley) and in avoiding death at the hands of his enemies. Sacrificial items, including a used gun cartridge carton and a cassowary claw, are about to be thrown into a fire as offerings.

Page 84   1975. Ongka butchers a pig killed as a sacrifice for this occasion.

Page 96   A Tipuka man of the Kitepi Kolkal sub-clan surveys the pigs at a moka. His head-dress includes a pair of hawk's wings (1970s).

Page 97   Ongka with his pig Rut Pepa, given away in the 1974 moka.

Page 98   The M.P. Parua-Kuri in modern dress poses with Ongka at the Maninge dance in 1971. Parua wears a Lions club cap, Ongka his 'mayoral' chain.

Page 99   Ongka dances in 1971 beside a clansman, Raema, who became his rival in 1974.

Page 100   Ongka discusses pigs with two old leaders of Membo clan, at an internal moka between Membo sub-clans.

Page 101   Ongka at a meeting with his father-in-law Ndamba (the father of Rumbukl) and others of Ndamba's sub-clan. Ongka visited Ndamba to ask for more pigs.

Page 102   1971. Ongka poses with his married daughter Ndau and his young daughter Yara, ready for the dance at Maninge.

Introduction

BIOGRAPHY AND PERSONHOOD

Biography and life-history narratives are among the sorts of materials that anthropologists cannot avoid gathering to one degree or another. Part of the business of collecting anthropological data is interviewing informants about their knowledge of specific topics that are relevant to the anthropologist's study, and each informant will bring to any topic a personal awareness of the "self" that is projected through the topic at hand. The extent to which an informant's biographical self projects into a discussion depends, of course, on the topic and the extent to which an informant routinely discusses his or her own history when providing explanatory comments. Thus, even when fieldworkers have gone into an area with the aim of specifically studying marriage patterns or burial practices, they will discover that they are also learning a great deal about the biographical aspects of the informants in their study.

Virginia Watson has recently (1996) published the life-history of the local translator, Anyan, with whom she worked in Tairora in the Eastern Highlands of Papua New Guinea. The translator had never sat down with Watson and specifically narrated her life-history but had over many months of work with Watson used examples from her own childhood, youth, and adult life to explain aspects of local social structure that seemed unclear to Watson. In fact, Watson did nothing with the specific details of Anyan's life-history until many years later when she gathered the materials together from various notebooks and published Anyan's life-history as a biographic work on its own. Watson had used Anyan's biographical examples over the years in her analysis of the Tairora people's culture in the broader sense. This is one of the main strengths of the use of life-history materials: They show us at the most intimate level how individuals fit (or do not fit) into the social structure they live within. Thus they help us understand how the society under study functions or responds to change.

The views of the society given by an important or respected woman will be different from those provided by a prostitute, as will those expressed by a leading male figure compared to a man who is an insignificant player in the political and ritual domains of life. But in all these instances biographical narratives explain aspects of how the various corners of the larger social unit function in historical circumstances (Stewart & Strathern, in press).

In the case of the materials furnished here, Ongka, a big-man or leader among the Kawelka people in the Mount Hagen area of Papua New Guinea sat and narrated in his own language, the Melpa language of Mount Hagen, his account of his life into a tape recorder with little prompting from an interviewer. He begins with early memories of childhood and his parents but doesn't follow a linear progression from birth to old age. Rather, he speaks about particular staging points within his life which he remembers as ones that transformed him in some way or another. Sometimes he begins a story at one point in time and shifts backwards or forwards in time as his mind pulls together the relevant bits to shape the story.

The narrative is thus neither linear nor cyclical but criss-crosses backwards and forwards in time in accordance with the play of Ongka's memory. He recalls vividly the precolonial times of childhood friendships and adult hostilities; the coming of the white people and the temporary ending of warfare, in which he attributes a strong role to himself; his *moka,* or exchange, activities, which culminated with his "big moka" of 1974; and what he sees as the decline, rather than upward movement, into independence. In 1995 he held essentially the same opinions, with more to substantiate them, given the turbulent political and social changes of the 1980s and 1990s. His ideas and feelings are thus expressed in a narrative that has a chronological shape overall, but the past easily blends with the present in his thoughts, and the whole narrative is not one of simple "development" toward an established end.

Many of Ongka's stories clearly illustrate what we have called the *relational-individual* (Strathern & Stewart, 1998a, 1998b; Stewart & Strathern, in press); that is, he clearly expresses himself as a person who has individual hopes and desires that are not always obtainable because of his particular embedded relationships with kin, enemies, or allies. Often his individual aims are only obtainable after a lengthy series of interactions or manipulations of those people with whom he has established particular sorts of relationships over time. As a leading male figure within his group he often saw himself as acting for the group as a whole, while at other times he saw his actions as solely maximizing his own gains in one particular arena or another. In an interesting passage early in his narrative (chap. 3), he tells of how he flouted traditional custom in order to pay special homage to his first wife, Pau, at the time of her funeral.

As Ongka discusses in chapter 14 of this book, many changes came during his lifetime as contact with European and Australian government officials and missionaries brought new goods, such as metal weapons and tools, and new ideas about many things to Papua New Guinea. All of these changes, such as ideas about ways of organizing government and new religious practices and ideals altered the ways that Ongka's people view themselves and their roles within the political and ritual life of their community. Many of the ways that the people cope with these changed circumstances are based on long-standing strategies that have proven successful in the past. In addition, new and creative techniques of coping are being developed all the time to meet the challenges of the moment and those that lie ahead. For example, social relations today occur on a very different scale in many ways from times past. Since groups are brought together in electorates, Council areas and provinces, the Hageners have tried to extend the principle of claiming and paying compensation on these new scales, for example between whole council areas, in order to settle conflicts. Such solutions in turn may generate new problems, for example, how to limit the size of demands for compensation payments at an interethnic level or between the people and the state. Entirely new techniques, based on Christian principles of forgiveness and reconciliation rather than the mediation of wealth, are being tried. These experiments also are having variable success.

From a wider analytical and theoretical angle, it is worthwhile to consider how life-history accounts such as Ongka's are pertinent to debates about some of the larger issues in cultural anthropology. Here we refer to the arguments about the linearity of notions of time, personal agency, and concepts of personhood which have been at the forefront of theorizing in cultural anthropology since the mid-1980s (see Marcus & Fischer [1986] for an early summary of these trends). Some have argued that we should beware of imposing linear structures of temporality since these are putatively Western and may not apply in Melanesian contexts. Asking people for life-histories may artificially impose such notions, it is argued. But there are dangers in this argument. First, it reduces a priori, rather than by way of evidence, the possibility of seeing similarities rather than differences cross-culturally, or of balancing similarities and differences. Second, asking for a life-history does not necessarily force linearity on the account provided the investigator refrains from attempting to introduce such a structure into the interviewing techniques used. In the present case no interviewing techniques were used at all, apart from an initial request that Ongka mention something about his childhood. The actual narrative often contains sections of historical ethnography, contemporary observations about geographical areas such as the Jimi Valley based on specialist knowledge, and opinions about life in general. Time in these accounts is neither linear nor cyclical. It exists simply as a background or component of the accounts themselves. There is a general division into the time before the white people, the time of the white people, and the time after the white people, but this, while providing a clear historical framework, is as episodic as it is linear.

With regard to issues of agency and personhood, it is curious that theorists on these topics since the mid-1980s have not made more extensive or more serious use of life-history materials, because these clearly show the concepts of personhood in the crucible of experience and history. The view that societies such as the Hagen society in the past did not have a concept of the individual and that this emerged only with modernity is in our opinion untenable on the basis of Ongka's narrative as well as materials from the very earliest ethnographic writers on the region (Vicedom & Tischner, 1943–1948; Strauss, 1962). Ongka certainly does not fit the Western type of an isolated citizen-subject who is not deeply enmeshed in ties of sociality and kinship. But Ongka, and others like him, are indeed convincing individuals. They trick others and are aware of being tricked. They act to impress themselves on others. They play truant from family tasks and then behave well to make up for it. They detect the malevolent intentions of others and thwart them. They explore new relationships for the possibilities they offer. They do all this not simply as generic human beings but in accordance with their own concepts of mind, intention, will, sympathy, anger, hostility, shame, and desire (many of which are encompassed in the meaning of the Hagen or Melpa term *noman*). Ongka's whole narrative has an aura of personal agency, and it is equally saturated with a sense of the collective, with an awareness of customs and traditions, with the meanings and values expressed in the implicit solidarities of kinship and marriage. In this way Ongka notably exemplifies the relational-individual outlook. The relational-individual is a universal category, not limited to the Hagen or any other society, but each society embraces its own combination, or package, of relational and individual values. Elucidating such complex packages, and why they exist, is difficult, more difficult than choosing difference or similarity as the leitmotiv of our analyses, but it is the major task we as anthropologists must bend our efforts to in the pursuit of cross-cultural humanity. One of the best ways to understand a society is to listen carefully to what its members have to say about it and to avoid overtheorizing, especially when the ethnographic data do not support a one-sided theoretical concept.

ONGKA, 1917–1997: FROM MBUKL TO KUK

Ongka's story was first narrated into a tape recorder set up for him in the prehistory laboratory at the University of Papua New Guinea in 1975. Later, he returned to his own place at Mbukl in the Highlands, flying back in a plane for only the second time in his life. As he got up to look out of one of the windows, he exclaimed, "Let's not do bad things!" meaning that the experience was both extraordinary and dangerous, and that behavioral taboos needed to be observed to make it safe. To ensure his own safety, the hostess then asked him to sit down and fasten his seat belt.

The home area that Ongka returned to was one that was just on the brink of Self-Government and later would become Independent. Prince Charles visited Papua New Guinea to take part in the Independence celebrations in September 1975. When he passed through Mount Hagen on a tour, Ongka was among those who met him and shook his hand, along with colonial officials such as Ron Hiatt and new indigenous politicians. Papua New Guinea was on a pathway of rapid change that would bring turbulence to many aspects of people's lives for many years to come.

Ongka, for his part, remained enmeshed in the exchanges of wealth goods that he delineates in such sharp detail in his narrative. As long as he continued to be based at Mbukl, he often visited his father-in-law, Ndamba, and observed the moka that Ndamba organized and both contributed and received gifts. By the 1980s, however, his interests took him more and more to his settlement at Poklök within the general area of Kuk, where the Kawelka had lived until early in the twentieth century. At that time they were driven out by the Mokei tribe and most took refuge down at Mbukl on the Sepik-Wahgi Divide on land neighboring that of the Tipuka tribe. The Kawelka had allied themselves with the Tipuka clansmen, but they were also involved in fighting them from time to time, as Ongka's narrative makes clear (chapter 6). His relocation from Mbukl to Poklök was aided by vehicles that he purchased with the help of contributions from many supporters (including K1,000 kina, at that time equivalent to USD $1000 from Andrew Strathern in recognition of the life-history that Ongka had narrated and its presentation in this book). At Poklök Ongka's family expanded its gardening areas in between the mountain ridge of Ep, where the fenced gardens resembled those on the hill slopes at Mbukl, and the drained flatlands of the recently established government agricultural research station. Two of his wives (Ruk and Kae) and their children were relocated first, while Rumbukl (the mother of Namba and Yara) remained largely at Mbukl near to the place of her father, Ndamba, who lived at Ngolke. Rumbukl often wanted to go to Kuk, whenever Ongka's car was due to make the journey, primarily to stake her claim to some of the prime garden land there but also to watch over the activities of her son, Namba, who was the driver of the car.

Over time, as the majority of the Kawelka shifted permanently to Kuk, the old ceremonial grounds at Maninge and Mbukl fell into disuse, and it was evident that the center of political affairs was no longer at Mbukl but back at Kuk, where Ongka's own father, Kaepa, had lived earlier in the century. By the 1980s Ongka's family had practically ceded their old settlement at Mbukl to growing numbers of people of the Tipuka Kitepi clan who lived around it. Visits to Mbukl in 1995 and 1997 confirmed that Mbukl, a Kawelka stronghold in the 1960s, had been entirely taken over by the Tipuka. A traditional-style round men's house belonging to a Tipuka leader (Wai, son of Nditing) stood where in colonial times a new-style "rest-house" for government officers on patrol had been built.

In addition to providing excellent garden land, Ongka's final shift of residence also had something to do with growing difficulties between himself and the Kitepi. His narrative depicts this relationship at a number of points (e.g., chapters 6, 10, 15). In chapter 15 he notes how as a result of the accidental death of a

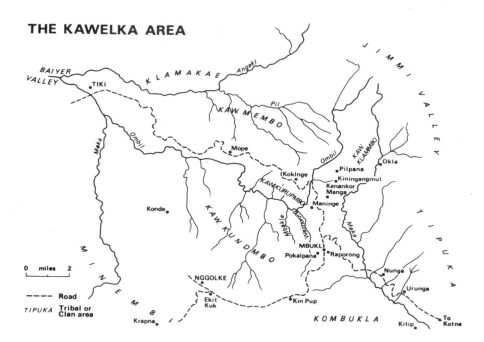

THE KAWELKA AREA

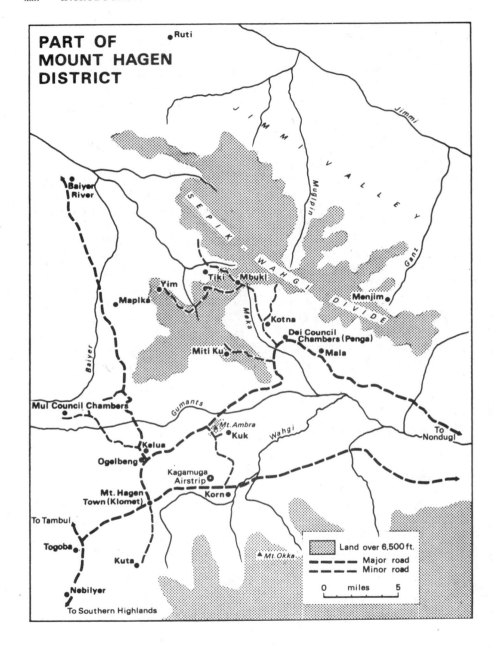

PART OF
MOUNT HAGEN
DISTRICT

Ruti

JIMMI VALLEY

Jimmi

Mugipin

Baiyer
River

SEPIK

WAHGI

Ganz

Tiki
Mbukl

Yim

Maplka

DIVIDE

Menjim

Baiyer

Meka

Kotna

Mitl Ku

Dei Council
Chambers (Penga)

Mala

Mul Council Chambers

Gumants

Mt. Ambra

Wahgi

To
Nondugl

Kelua

Kuk

Ogelbeng

Kagamuga
Airstrip

Mt. Hagen
Town (Klomet)

Korn

To Tambul

Togoba

Kuta

▲ Mt. Okka

Nebilyer

To Southern Highlands

Land over 6,500 ft.

Major road

Minor road

0   miles   5

Kitepi man named Wonom in Port Moresby he was made a target of accusations and placed in a dangerous situation like that resulting earlier from a dispute over the death of Nggaep, a Kitepi leader or big-man who was the son of the preeminent leader Kuri described in chapter 10). The Kitepi lived all around Ongka at Mbukl. After being constrained to make a compensation payment to them, he may have realized that his life would be more secure if he abandoned Mbukl and went back to his father's original place. There was even less to keep him at Mbukl after Parua, another of Kuri's sons and a Member of Parliament had organized the return moka for the large gift Ongka orchestrated in 1974 (see chapter 13). There were complaints over this, and the exchange-based alliance between the groups as a whole faltered and began to run out of support. The alliance received another, and perhaps fatal, blow from an event that occurred not in the Hagen area itself but in Port Moresby in 1988. The son of a Kawelka big-man of the Membo clan, was struck down with a stick in a brawl outside the house of a Kitepi man (who happened to be married to a Kawelka woman) behind the Administrative College (now the Public Service Training Institute) in the suburb of Waigani in Port Moresby. The attack happened during the night, and no one reported it till morning, when the victim was found dead. The Kitepi man was arrested and jailed for the killing. The Kitepi clansmen later paid a sum of K12,000 and a large number of pigs as a customary compensation for this killing, but it was rumored that the real killer had not been found, and the compensation did not seem to heal the social rupture caused by the death as it was supposed to do. The dead man came from the clan of the mother of the Member of Parliament Parua-Kuri, and Parua himself was the product of a moka gift from the Kawelka to his father, his mother having been given in marriage as a gift to Kuri in a precolonial moka presentation. Thus the killing was a negation of an alliance that had begun with a gift of a life. This marriage-based alliance had in any case been shaken by two further circumstances: a parliamentary political rivalry and a resurgent pattern of intergroup warfare near Mbukl, both of which reached a climax in the mid-1980s.

The loss of exchange partnerships and possibilities is central in this story. Warfare in the 1980s scattered most of Ndamba's kin in many directions, although he himself clung tenaciously to his old settlement, even as late as 1997. Ongka thereby lost the basis for pursuing his extended *moka* ties with Ndamba's group in the vicinity of Mbukl. The attenuation of the exchange-alliance with the Kitepi was influenced by, and influenced, a rift at the level of modern politics. In elections up to and through the 1970s the Kawelka had fairly solidly supported the Tipuka M.P. Parua and thereby ensured his reelection. In the 1980s, however, this pattern changed as Kawelka political interests shifted. The earlier political alliance had been based largely on physical propinquity and the marriage of the Kitepi leader Kuri and his Kawelka Membo wife Nomane. In other words, the early phases of electoral politics were grounded fairly squarely on the politics of residential alliance and moka exchange. But later phases diverged from this pattern. Given the sizes of groups and the adoption of a first-past-the-post system of voting in which the candidate who gained the greatest number of votes won the election and no secondary or tertiary preference votes were cast, it became evident that the preeminence of the Tipuka depended not only on continued Kawelka support but also on the votes of groups that were enemies of the Kawelka, among the Kombukla and Minembi tribes. Attempts by Parua-Kuri, and later his son, Reuben, to secure support from these groups did not meet with much approval from his traditional allies. At the same time younger Kawelka men began also to build alliances with politicians supported by the Kombukla and Minembi, bringing them into opposition to Parua-Kuri's family.

The situation was complicated further by the fierce warfare between the Kawelka as a whole and various clans of the Minembi tribe that broke out after a single killing in the 1980s. A not unusual case, the incident was the result of carousing and beer drinking that led to fisticuffs and an apparently unintended fatal injury (see Strathern, 1993a, chapter 4). In this case the death of a young Kawelka clansman called Palyim at the hands of neighboring Minembi Yelipi men was followed by a refusal to pay compensation. This led the Kawelka to resolve to fight the Minembi and call on their allies for help. The Tipuka, however, did not come to their aid en masse, and the Kawelka, especially the Kundmbo, suffered accordingly; thus, the Kawelka took their revenge on weaker and more vulnerable Minembi groups.

The war that thus took shape in the mid-1980s unsettled the Kawelka at Kuk badly, but it was disastrous for those near Mbukl who were in the front lines of attack from the Minembi. These included chiefly the Kundmbo at Ngolke and some Membo clansfolk living adjacent to the Andakelkam, a section of the Minembi near Tiki plantation (see Ongka's account in chapter 15 for forerunner events in relation to this group of Minembi and the Klamakae). The Membo clan as a whole was not immediately involved in the war, but they were pulled into it as a result of deaths caused by the Andakelkam. Later, in accordance with cultural rules, the two Kawelka clans primarily involved had to pay out a large compensation to the Membo, which was completed in 1991. All other allies, from tribes whose members had individually helped the Kawelka, also had to be paid in the inexorable balancing of wealth against death that shadows any warfare.

In all of these events Ongka was fully involved, in making contributions and speeches, but it was clear by the 1990s that he was growing very tired of both the physical dangers of war and the heavy obligations of compensation payments. In 1974 he had thought that modernity would bring an end to the *moka* because the younger generation of Kawelka at both Mbukl and Kuk had different motives and habits. His 1974 *moka* was intended as his last big show (chapter 13). He did not then anticipate the outbreaks of tribal violence that the 1980s would bring, which would necessitate another wearying round of compensation payments.

In his narrative (e.g., chapter 10) Ongka strikes a very confident tone in describing his ability to intimidate people and to thwart those who tried to kill him. He describes how his actions, marked by a certain kind of excess, served to reinforce the imposition of colonial rule and the "ending" (or rather, temporary cessation) of warfare. By the mid-1980s his confidence was gone. Warfare was back, made worse by the use of guns. Ongka himself was shaken by a physical attack in 1985, which led to a complicated internal inquiry by a "trouble committee" and a payment of compensation to him. He was no longer able to control events, either within the Kawelka or externally, as he had done for a while in the heyday of the colonial administration by his adroit use of the *moka* and his occupation of official roles, from boss-boy to local government councilor. From the time of his effective transfer to Kuk, he had voluntarily retired from the position of councilor for all the Kawelka, thus absolving himself of the burden of overseeing matters at both Mbukl and Kuk. In 1989 he took a further step to remove himself from politics by entering into baptism in the Catholic Church at Kuk, announcing that this signified his retirement from the politics of war and compensation and preparation for his eventual death.

By the end of 1995 Ongka had suffered many losses: all of his wives were dead other than Mande, whom he had acquired during his preparations for the moka of 1974 (chapter 13) and Kae, who was the mother of his son Keni. In addition, his son Namba died in September 1995 of heart disease (mitral valve prolapse), leaving a wife and five children behind. His married daughter, Yara, came with her two daughters to stay at Poklök and look after him as well as the grave of her mother, Rumbukl, who had died of breast cancer in 1992. Ongka took Namba's body and buried it down at Mbukl at the head of the old ceremonial ground he had laid out for the *moka* of 1974. Not really able to retire from politics, he had played his part in arranging the compensation for a killing in 1995 that threatened the stability of the Kawelka's occupation of land at Kuk. In 1996 he suffered a stroke, from which he recovered but needed medicine to reduce his blood pressure and combat anemia. Still full of fiery energy on occasion, and as manipulative as ever, he sought in 1997 to raise a bride-wealth for his last son, David, by his favorite wife, Rumbukl. In doing so, he grumbled that now at the end of his own life he had to try and play the role of "both mother and father," but this was not truly possible. His own narrative makes clear at a number of points (chapters 4, 13) that he realized that men may claim prestige but they depend on women for work, support, and organization. Left on his own in his late old age, he felt insufficient and in the end incomplete. His life lived with men had been dependent on his life lived with women. In 1999 we learned that he had given directions that at his death he should be buried at Mbukl next to his son Namba, in order to protect the long-term interests of the Kawelka in their land there.

POLITICS AND WARFARE

The personal events of Ongka's life were inextricably bound up with political relations. He himself left a strong mark on those relations over time. His stroke in 1996 offers a dramatic illustration. It was brought on after he heard that one of his sons, who is now an assistant in the Catholic Church, knocked out another man of his own subclan with a stick in a conflict over the use of some planks, an event that required a compensation payment later. Ongka collapsed on hearing the news and was taken to the hospital and given blood transfusions from several donors, male and female, in his immediate family and within the Kawelka group. These gestures clearly showed that Ongka was a respected individual and leader. As had happened after the attack on Ongka in the 1980s, many people commented on his historic role among the Kawelka as a small group surrounded by stronger tribes.

At that time in the mid 1980s the threat of fighting between the Kawelka and the Minembi people prompted the Kawelka to solicit help from allies who would assist them in opposing their numerically much stronger foes. The Kawelka at Kuk felt obliged to send off their men to assist their tribesmen at Mbukl, and truckloads of fighters left the Raiorong ceremonial ground aiming to proceed at night by circuitous routes up to Mbukl and join in the fighting there. There were rumors that the Minembi, with Kombukla allies, were advancing southwards over the Ep mountain ridge at the back of Ongka's place, Poklök, and might descend on the major Kawelka settlements at dawn while most of their men were away at Mbukl. Such rumors periodically caused panic and preparations for flight, and Ongka was involved in steadying people and planning strategic responses to the Minembi threat. He also played a leading part in a meeting held in front of the Female Spirit cult grove where the men due to go out to fight the next day were all asked to reveal any wrongdoings or grudges. Such hidden problems must be aired, the Kawelka believe, to ensure ancestral support and to reduce the likelihood of betrayals that could keep the battle from being successful. Ongka here was reenacting a precolonial ritual role of the big-man (see also A.J. Strathern, 1993a, 1993b).

The Kawelka generally were in a weak position. Divided in their territorial location, they found it impossible to defend both territories at once. Fortunately, the Minembi warriors did not make it as far as Poklök, and Ongka and others were spared. This period of warfare profoundly altered the political landscape of the wider area, however. No compensations for killings were paid between the Minembi and the Kawelka, so that the enmity between them remained in place, although a Christian cross planted at their border marked a peace between them. The lack of compensation payments in turn ensured their continued competition in the modern political arena.

Rivalry for the position of the member of Parliament acted like a magnet to shape the force fields of politics in the region. To a considerable extent, this was due to the fact that the national-level MPs came to command an inordinate amount of political leverage, not so much through their parliamentary work as such, but rather through their discretionary powers to disburse sectoral allocation funds for development in their electorates. These powers, and the amounts of money available to each MP, as well as the rules of accountability attached to them, have varied over time, but the sums involved have invariably been considerable and therefore an object of competition and jealousy within the electorates. The amounts of money have reached at times K750,000 per MP each year, enabling MPs to engage in obvious forms of patronage politics, including attempts to purchase the votes needed for their reelection. Such attempts are by no means always successful since their opponents also offer bribes to supporters, and there are always disgruntled factions who feel they have been excluded from the MP's largesse. In addition, the tribal boundaries, which became somewhat hardened after the warfare of the 1980s, have made it more difficult to bribe successfully across them.

It is scarcely surprising that reports of "electoral violence" have appeared in analyses of electoral behavior in the PNG Highlands (Saffu, 1996). In particular, disgruntled citizens, whose candidate failed to win after they gave bribes to outsiders, tend to attack those whose votes they thought they had secured and whom they subsequently suspect of voting for another candidate. In addition, the candidate who wins is thought to have done so only by some trick—an understandable response given the rather even matching of candidates in terms of the group support they command and the small margins by which victories are often won. Ongka summed up this attitude in explaining how a surprising candidate had won the 1997 election in Dei council. It was a case like that of the *kimbukla opra,* the water-snake, he said. When fishermen catch a large number of fish in their net they are happy, but when they draw the net up they may see that the fish have disappeared. Then they see the water-snake, distended, lying at the bottom of the net. They realize that the snake has eaten all the fish. In the same way, Ongka said, the other candidates were sure that they had captured votes, but when the ballot papers were counted it was found that the winner had swallowed everyone else's votes. The implication is that the winner had somehow arranged for a large number of votes to be cast for him inside his own local stronghold, perhaps by enrolling coffee plantation workers from elsewhere as residents.

In 1995 the Kawelka became embroiled in a confrontation with the Mokei people over a killing. Two young Kawelka men got into a barroom brawl with a Mokei man, and the latter was struck with a piece of metal pipe and died from the blow. The Mokei, short of land since some of their territory had been taken for the urban expansion of Mount Hagen Township, asked the Kawelka for land in compensation. Pik-Ruin, a Kawelka who had been the deputy premier of the provincial government in Western Highlands Province until the national Parliament dissolved all provincial governments, emerged as a leader in the negotiations with the Mokei over this issue (see the film *A Death To Pay For* and the accompanying book of interview materials [Strathern & Stewart, 1998b]). Pik used his efforts in this conflict as a basis for uniting the Kawelka behind him in a bid for a national MP position in 1997. His prime opponent was sitting MP Reuben-Parua of Tipuka Kitepi, who had defeated Melchior-Pep, a Kombukla politician, in a by-election after challenging the 1992 election results. Pik had previously assisted Melchior. His challenge to Reuben marked the further dissolution of the old Tipuka-Kawelka alliance, but the Kawelka were left with no immediate returns for their expensive campaign as well as the certainty that the Tipuka would resent Pik's intervention, which may have removed needed votes from Reuben himself. The winner, Puri-Ruing, profited from these divisions. He seems to have had no alliance ties with the Kawelka at all. Pik contented himself with becoming elected later in 1997 as one of the local government councilors in a new political structure designed to give back to councils powers previously exercised (since 1979) through the provincial governments.

The Kawelka had other difficulties too. They had moved onto abandoned government station land at Kuk in order to cope with their growing land shortages and were uncertain of how this move would be regarded by the government, especially since they had no effective ties with the new MP. Land in the High-lands of Papua New Guinea is at a premium because of the importance of coffee as a cash crop and the growth in overall population, and its significance as a basis of power has become more transparently evident with the slow decline of the old indigenous exchange system, the *moka,* and its replacement by isolated, unilateral compensation payments for killings between groups. *Moka* exchanges in the past, as Ongka's narrative makes clear (e.g., chapter 13), created and fostered alliance ties between groups, which were based on reciprocal exchanges over time. These alliance ties have diminished in response to modern hostilities and the younger generation's loss of interest in the old customs of work and display (also clearly pointed out by Ongka). Urban-based behavior has brought a rise of interest in consumerism and a desire for quick access to money and goods, which finds expression in the criminal behavior of gangs but also in people's daily visits to town to sell foods in the market or buy goods in the stores. Thieves roam the streets of the town by day, pilfering stray goods from the backs of trucks and slitting open locked doors on vehicles to seize shopping items. By night there are concerted, armed attacks on gas stations and security headquarters. The police are hard pressed to control the streets and to prevail in shoot-outs with nocturnal gang robbers. Ongka in 1974 was not very sanguine about the future prospects for his country, but he did not perceive the degree to which problems of law and order would emerge with the development of social classes, the desire for goods, and the decline of behavior patterns associated with respect and shared values between the generations.

Assessing the contribution of national and international influences to changes in daily life in Hagen is not a very easy task. The Papua New Guinea state, and its constitution, is in a sense an international product; at the same time it seeks to create and build on a sense of the nation to underpin the authority of its institutions. The rules of criminal justice governing killings exemplify one context in which indigenous and introduced ideas have clearly clashed. At the same time it is equally obvious—and made clear in Ongka's own account—from the 1930s onward that local leaders have been willing to be co-opted into the state project of producing persons as individuals subject to the law, even as the forces of kinship and local politics have created resistance to this project. Most of the time, things get done in Hagen through a complex mixture of processes that have their origins in various time periods. Disputes, for example, are heard by Village Court magistrates, but often in informal "moot" contexts, and the ideas used to settle conflicts always entail some element of emphasis on compensatory payments, even if a failure to comply may be met by a jail order.

In this complicated arena it has become increasingly evident throughout the 1990s that one set of influences has grown enormously: the voices of church leaders of various denominations. During 1998 the old issue of polygyny again became a focus of church criticism, but unlike in colonial times when native custom was allowed to hold sway in the domestic realms of kinship and marriage and in the village courts, the churches this time have decided to mount their campaign at a national level. Using both legal and political arguments, based on the principles of Christianity and human rights, they are pressuring Parliament to make a law against polygyny. If polygyny is abolished, there will in future be no productive basis for the power of big-men such as Ongka nor any reason to articulate this power by forming material alliances through marriage and exchange.

RELIGION AND CHANGE

Christian missions first came into the region where Ongka has lived in the 1930s. Catholic and Lutheran missionaries built churches, provided health services, and tried to teach the local people about Christianity while also learning and often recording the languages and customs of the people. These missions, like the Pentecostal missions that were to follow in the 1960s, found that many of the local customs were not in conformity with particular church doctrines. Each church condemned or tolerated various practices, which over time influenced people in their decisions to join one church or another or to stay out of the church altogether. Various political and ritual practices were targeted by missionaries as ones which they thought should be altered or eliminated from the cultural life of the people. The Kor Wöp (Male Spirit cult) and Amb Kor (Female Spirit cult) rituals were condemned in this way. The competitive exchange system of *moka* was not supported by the churches and the practice of polygyny was not encouraged. Often, if a man wanted to join a church, he was forced to say that he had set all his other wives aside and had only retained one whom he could then bring to the church with him for Sunday service. This, of course, produced many difficulties for the other wives, who were not really sent away but who felt ashamed and jealous that they were not the one who was selected as the official wife. Some churches such as the Assemblies of God (AOG) allow a man with more than one wife to bring all his wives to church with him, realizing that to do otherwise produces additional domestic hostilities on top of the many that already exist in the polygamous household. The AOG, like other churches, encourages monogamous marriages and supports individuals who have a church marriage prior to or instead of bride-price payments. There is also a movement among religious organizations within Papua New Guinea to seek legislation that makes polygamy illegal.

These ideological changes, which profoundly affect social practices, represent just a few of the many changes that have been occurring as the country modernizes. In fact, some people have identified the confusing circumstances in which they live with the signs described in the Book of Revelations and believe that the end of the world is at hand. These end-time beliefs were heightened in 1997 and 1998 with the effects of the severe drought and subsequent flooding in the area induced by El Niño. These harsh climatic conditions have contributed to the spread of infectious diseases, which many have viewed as another sign of the end.

As for Ongka, he told us in 1997 that his people had prayed for his recovery and had donated their blood to him. He himself had asked God to give him just three more years, so that he could survive until the millennium, when he hoped he would have a megaphone to use to tell his people which way to go. In mid-1998 he was more hopeful about the future. Encouraged by the return of fertility to the ground, he assured us that he did not intend to die and would see us the following year.

YARA

Like her father, Yara is a person with a strong individual character. She consciously models herself on both of her parents. At the same time, she is critical of her father on certain issues, such as his refusal to send her to school, which she links to gender biases in the Hagen society. Yara's accounts of herself, her relations with her parents, and her ideas about her society and the churches' end-time messages are given in the last part of this book as a counterpoint and supplement to Ongka's own narrative. Blocked from directly succeeding Ongka as a leader because of social restrictions on her gender, Yara has made good use of more recent Christian messages to carve out for herself a niche as an interpreter of dreams. She also uses her own dreams as a means of legitimizing her access to special knowledge (much as Hagen males have done in the past in relation to the Female and Male Spirit cults) and status in the Christian scheme of things. She narrates her own dreams as prophetic indications for herself and her community and also interprets the Christian significance of dreams for others. Yara's account marks the latest attempt by the Hageners to adapt outside influences to local social relations and to create patterns that can bring advantages to enterprising individuals, while drawing on the new forms of church life in the Christian mode.

REFERENCES

Marcus, G. & M. Fischer. (1986). *Anthropology as cultural critique. An experimental moment in the social sciences.* Chicago: University of Chicago Press.

Saffu, Y. (Ed.). (1996). *The 1992 PNG election: Change and continuity in electoral politics.* Canberra: Australian National University.

Stewart, P. J., & Strathern, A. J. (Eds.) (in press). Identity work: Constructing Pacific lives. *ASAO Monograph Series, 18.* University of Pittsburgh Press.

Strathern, A. J. (1993a). Voices of conflict. *Ethnology Monographs, 14.* Pittsburgh: Department of Anthropology, University of Pittsburgh.

———. (1993b). Violence and political change in Papua New Guinea. *Pacific Studies, 16*(4), 41–60.

Strathern, A. J., & Stewart, P. J. (1998a). Seeking personhood: Anthropological accounts and local concepts in Mount Hagen, Papua New Guinea. *Oceania 68*(3), 170–188.

———. (1998b). *A death to pay for: Individual voices.* Pittsburgh: Department of Anthropology, University of Pittsburgh. Distributed by Pennsylvania State University Media Services.

Strauss, H. & H. Tischner. (1962). *Die Mi-Kultur der Hagenberg-Stämme.* Hamburg: Cram, de Gruyter & Co.

Vicedom, G. F. & H. Tischner. (1943–1948). *Die Mbowamb* (3 vols.) Hamburg: Friederichsen, de Gruyter & Co.

Watson, V. (1996). *Anyan's story: A New Guinea woman in two worlds.* Seattle: University of Washington Press.

1 / A Thunderclap Gone Mad

Let me tell you the story of how I was born, as my father told it to me. It was at Raporong, down from my present home, Mbukl, at the time when two of our Kawelka men[1] were killed in warfare by Kombukla tribesmen, that my mother bore me. My father was on his way home in the rain when my mother felt the pain come on. His two men had been killed and the people were at the funeral, and so he called me "Ongka." He thought, "The Kombukla have killed my men, what can I do to kill one of them in return?" and he called me Ongka after the adz which we use to shape and sharpen our weapons, as he thought about revenge. He told me about this later when I was old enough to listen.

So I began to grow up, crawling around at first, and when I was big enough I caught grasshoppers and other jumping insects among the sweet potato leaves in the gardens. I and my friends used also to spit grubs which bored into trees, singing a song to the grubs as we did so. We would not go far from home, for everywhere around us there was warfare and my father warned us that we might be killed. He told us to stick to the edges of streams in our own territory, and there we ran, catching lizards and tadpoles.

Later when I grew a bit bigger, I thought, "Why am I spending all my time beside the streams? I'll go off and have a look at the forest now." I asked my father to make a bow for me so I could go hunting small birds. The white men had not come at that time; we had to make things with stone tools, with just ordinary stones! We had to cut and shape them on sandstones, dipping them in water and rubbing them till our hands were blistered and sore. We took these ax blades and struck at trees with them, but the blades were blunt and glanced off the trunk. Only strong men could finish the task of cutting a tree down; weak men had to give up. Often we were hungry, too, when we worked. Well, my father made a bow and arrows for me, and I cut myself some branches to make a bird-blind. I had a pronged arrow strung ready and waited for birds to come. When I got my first bird I was delighted. Another thing we did was to take long sticks and push these up into the debris of leaves and rubbish in pandanus trees,[2] where marsupials hid. When one fell down we seized it and exclaimed over its size, feeling we had caught something so much bigger than frogs or grubs, and so we went to the forest regularly in search of game. I continued hunting in the forest until I grew older and taller and grease came to my face[3] and I thought, "Why am I in the forest all

---

[1] Their names were Kur and Ik, both of Membo clan.
[2] (Ongka refers here to the nut pandanus tree, which has thick, spiky leaves in which rubbish gathers.)
[3] (This is a sign of adolescence.)

KAWELKA TRIBE

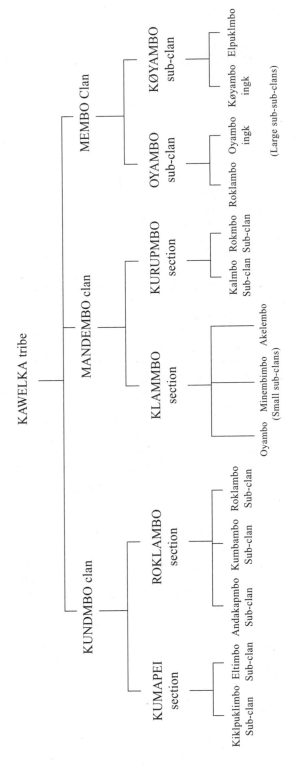

KAWELKA tribe

MANDEMBO clan — MEMBO Clan

KUNDMBO clan

KUMAPEI section
- Kiklpuklimbo Sub-clan
- Eltimbo Sub-clan

ROKLAMBO section
- Andakapmbo Sub-clan
- Kumbambo Sub-clan
- Roklambo Sub-clan

KLAMMBO section (Small sub-clans)
- Oyambo
- Minembimbo
- Akelembo

KURUPMBO section
- Kalmbo Sub-clan
- Rokmbo Sub-clan

OYAMBO sub-clan
- Roklambo
- Oyambo ingk

KØYAMBO sub-clan
- Køyambo ingk
- Elpuklmbo ingk

(Large sub-sub-clans)

(1) Ongka himself belongs to the small Oyambo sub-clan within Klammbo section of Mandembo clan.

(2) Marriage within the clan is prohibited; but there is a considerable degree of intermarriage within the tribe.

the time hunting birds?" I saw other boys joining in the courting sessions with young girls whose big breasts and looks I liked, and so I went courting too. Playing and joking with the girls, taking part with them in games of throwing mud, I forgot about the times when I hunted for birds. I visited girls' houses, playing, singing courting songs to them, taking food from their mothers, until I thought, "I could get one of them in marriage, but what can I give in bride-wealth to get one of them?" My father was an old man by that time, but he put a bride-wealth payment together and obtained my first wife for me. One of the things he used was brought by the white men. When the first planes of the white men came, I was down by a stream. There were several of us, old men and young boys, all working at shaping stone axes. I thought I heard the voice of one of those marsupials that growl as they go along and have tails like lizards' tails.[4] We chased the noise through the undergrowth; it kept moving in front of us and we couldn't catch it. Then we looked up and saw it was in the sky and we said, "It's a kind of witch-craft[5] come to strike us and eat us up!" We argued about it: was it really witch-craft, or was it a big hornbill bird or an eagle? Some said it was a thunderclap gone mad and come down from the sky. Then it went away and we said we would find out about it later.

We did not know it had landed at Hagen.[6] There were so many wars between groups all the way from us to Hagen, how could we go to see? Eventually someone did go all the way and returned to tell us that a foreign man with plenty of wealth in shells had set up a house of barkcloth[7] at Kelua near to Ogelbeng. He had come down in the flying thing and was living there. Later we saw Jim Taylor himself.[8] He came through and called out for supplies for his many carriers. People took sugarcane, sweet potatoes, bananas, and pigs to him. He would draw out of his long trouser pockets a big mottled cowrie shell of the kind we valued, and show it to them, and they said, "Oh! He has a big cowrie and he's drawn it out of his own behind!" That was how we got to know the white man. When I was a boy, before these men came, we had a very hard time. My father told me how to do things, and it was all hard work. We used a sharpened stick as a bushknife to cut down stands of cane and grass. Every piece for our stone axes—the balancer, the thongs for binding, the handle, and the blade—we had to fashion for ourselves. There were only a few sources of the blades, mostly in the forests of the Jimi, and the grassland people who had no sources of their own used to take their girls and their big pigs and give them away in return for axes. So the axes were exchanged from hand to hand and passed out as far as the Enga people to our west.[9] If a man

---

[4] (The animal is called *Kui koklum* in Melpa.)

[5] (Witchcraft, *kum,* is said to be able to fly through the air, appearing at night as a bright light.)

[6] (Where the town of Mount Hagen was later built, some 20 to 30 miles from the Kawelka tribe's territory to its south.)

[7] (A tent.)

[8] (Taylor was one of the first explorers of the Highlands, who first came to Hagen along with two of the Leahy brothers, Mick and Dan, in 1933. The latter were gold prospectors, while Taylor was a government officer.)

[9] The Maplke, Palke, Kitingambo, Mongaepkae, and Oklmone—these were the groups who made the various kinds of axes and sent them out of the Jimi Valley southwards to the Ndika,

had a daughter and was brought a bride-wealth of ten axes in payment for her, he was delighted and said, "The ax man has come to get our girl!" They gave wives especially to the ax manufacturers, for they preferred these axes even beyond pigs and shells, saying how one's hands blistered in making them. "Pigs and shells are all right," they said, "but give me axes so I can work, make gardens, and eat food." If you asked for a wife and promised an ax, you would be sure to get her; if you wanted someone killed and promised an ax to their assassin, you could be sure the killing would be done.

In the past we used long wooden sticks for a spade. We dug ditches, the men holding the spades, the women getting down into the trench and pulling up the lumps of earth with their hands. Then Taylor brought us real spades, knives, and axes, and cowrie shells as well. After him came Michael and Dan Leahy, who lived at Kuta, sluicing the river for gold and paying people with shells too. One day two men from that area[10] brought some of the large new cowrie shells down to Mbukl. One of them had the name Kuta Wak. I was away in the nearby Jimi Valley at courting sessions when my father met the men and offered them a big pig in return for this special shell with the name. I heard about the visit of these strangers on my way back home, and I later asked my father why he had given away his finest big pig to get the shell Kuta Wak. He said, "Don't say anything about it! Pigs are things that we eat up and leave their bones in the cult houses dedicated to the spirits. It doesn't matter!" But I was thinking of how one of the new steel axes could slice right through a tree, and I was cross and said, "Why did you get a worthless shell? With a steel ax think of the work we could do." Then my father told me to be quiet, for he had bought the cowrie in order to obtain a wife for me. I said, "I don't want a wife, I want a steel ax," and we had a big row about it. "You have no wife," he said. "Don't you know I want to get one for you? The white men are here and they'll be bringing plenty more axes for you; now this special shell is for your bride." "I don't want a bride, I want an ax," I repeated. However, the men led the pig away and I said no more about it, and so my father got me a wife.

At this time some of the clans of the Tipuka tribe had begun fighting among themselves. The Kitepi, Oklembo, Ndikambo, and Wanyembo, all those who lived at the head of the Möka River, fought on one side, and all those who lived along its middle reaches, the Kengeke and Kendike and the Papeke and Yelipi clans of Minembi tribe fought against them. I was just a boy—my head hair had been cropped—but I took cane inflorescences and grasses and put them in my hair as a battle decoration, and went to help the headwater groups whose girls I had been courting. I helped them a great deal; the enemies were so keen to kill me they brought bunches of spears into battle to aim at me, but they couldn't kill me. I closed the doors against the enemies, and the people were so grateful they said

---

Yamka, Keme, and Kukilika. The axe types were called *tinggrina, ketepukla, wonopa, ranggeklip, kraep, yambina, kontin,* and *nggaema.* We Kawelka had our own *mbukl* blades and the Tipuka, our neighbors, had the *pukl.* The Kuli-Kele of the Waghi Valley had the blades called *kumbamong.* These were the only groups who made axes.

[10] A Kuma Kope and a Penambe Wiyambo man.

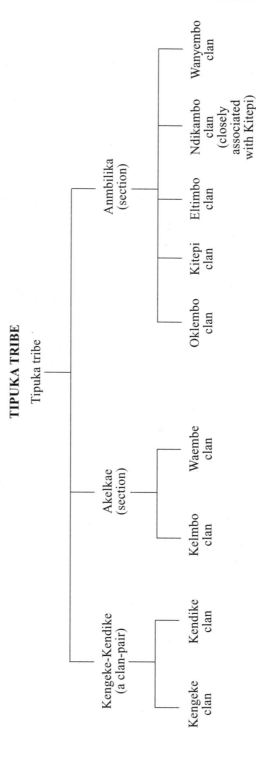

TIPUKA TRIBE

Tipuka tribe

Kengeke-Kendike (a clan-pair)

Kengeke clan

Kendike clan

Akelkae (section)

Kelmbo clan

Waembe clan

Anmbilika (section)

Oklembo clan

Kitepi clan

Eltimbo clan

Ndikambo clan (closely associated with Kitepi)

Wanyembo clan

(1) Ongka's most important exchange-partner, the M.P. Parua-Kuri, belongs to one of the sub-clans (not shown here) of Kitepi clan in Anmbilika section.

(2) As with the Kawelka, intra-clan marriage is prohibited; but Tipuka clans marry freely among themselves, and with Kawelka.

they would give me a wife for nothing; my father was just to bring one pig and the big cowrie shell. In fact my father gave eight pigs, the special cowrie, and also a mat of nassa shells,[11] and so I married an Oklembo clanswoman, the woman Pau, who became the mother of my eldest daughter, Raem.

After this I began to think how I was to get one of the new axes. An old man of the Yamka tribe from Kelua, called Yaklaka, came to our place and I asked to go back with him. At this time the first kiap who had made his place at Klomet was Master Murray.[12] I went to Kelua and from there I walked down to Klomet with a bundle of vegetables on my back, and there I saw how people were getting two cowrie shells for a bagful of food and one shell for an amount of thatching grass. Those who wanted it could get small amounts of decorating paint[13] poured out for them. So there they all were, getting cowries and face-paint and knives with edges so sharp!

People from the Minembi tribe, fifteen to twenty miles away, were trying to get through with loads of food to trade, but their enemies the Yamka caught them, made fools of them, and slaughtered them with their axes.[14] Some of the bodies their kinsmen managed to take off and bury, but others were left there in the grasslands and the hawks ate them. In this way many people from the forest areas were being killed when they tried to cross the grasslands, so the Minembi shuddered and said, "All right, let the Yamka have those things for themselves!" One woman Kuk, who died, was wife of Nambakae Ndopaem, and the family used to live high up on the slopes of the hill known as Miti Ku. She was killed over at Kelua and her husband and children sitting at home did not know how to get over there and see after they heard the news. Holding his orphaned children to him the husband sang his lament in their forest place:

Woman Kuk over at Weip
She picked and strung
Her nassa shells
She picked and strung
Her tambu shells
Weip woman Kuk
Did she go to sleep
In the house of cloth[15] at Kelua?

The white men were angry with the Yamka for this and put them in jail for it. Jim Taylor made them dig up earth and put it in bags and carry it around and

---

[11] (Large numbers of tiny shells sewn onto a kind of barkcloth backing.)

[12] (Probably Murray Edwards, stationed in Mount Hagen from around 1936 to 1938. "Kiap" means government officer.) The true name of the place was *pokapokl num,* since there was a pond there where people went to catch frogs of the kind called *pokapokl.* Where the subprovince office now is was called Pongönt Kona, where the Mokei Pangamb people lived. The old airstrip was a swamp full of cane-grass and frogs, and the place where the hospital now is was called Ndapeorong. (In Hagen every small locality has its name, and here Ongka details the old locality names now replaced by parts of the modern town.)

[13] (Powder that could be mixed with water and used in face-painting for festivals, in colors of blue, red, and yellow, replacing earth-paints traditionally employed for this purpose.)

[14] Nambakae Maep and Yelipi Parka and a woman called Kuk were killed in this way.

[15] (The white men's tent, near to which she was killed.)

around all day as a punishment, until they were really tired of it. The Minembi also took their revenge. A Minembi man[16] stole over at night to the place of the Yamka leader, Kaukla, and killed him, and this provoked battle between them, until they were tired of this and separated, saying, "Let's not fight, war is a rubbish way of doing things," and so they stopped of their own will.

The white men also jailed two Minembi men and a Römndi tribesman[17] for punishing a woman by burning her genitals.[18] The woman was a little woman of the Mokei tribe married to the Römndi man. She died, and her kinsfolk were angry at her death and at other deaths they had suffered at the hands of the same group, so they reported it to the kiap, who came and took the men away and had them beaten to death and buried secretly in the jail place. When the people heard this, oh, they recoiled as snails do into their shells when someone touches them with a burning stick! The kiap had taken those three big men away and killed them, and their burial places could not be found; some said they were still in jail, some that they had been killed and sent off in a plane, some that they had been hidden underneath the ground. Then the people who talked of killing others by fighting were very frightened. They searched and searched for the graves, all the wives and sons of these men joined in the search, but they couldn't find them. They said, "The white man will kill us all if we don't give up fighting. We must give up this rubbish habit of making war." And so warfare was stopped in the area.

When Master Murray went away Master George came.[19] He saw me once when I was involved in stopping a fight and he told me he would make me a "boss boy."[20] I said, "What? I'm only a boy! I would be ashamed to stand up and speak in front of the big-men who have been leaders in fighting and killed people in the past." "That doesn't matter," he replied. "You've been bold enough to come and speak in front of me, so I'm making you a boss boy." He gave me a cane stick as a sign of my position and told me to stop trouble and fighting. If a man had intercourse with another man's wife, I was to extract payment from the adulterer in order to "tie up the woman's apron."[21] He told me to beat the woman with my cane and tell her not to do it again; if the guilty man refused to pay the compensation, I was to bring him into the government station where he would be jailed by the Kiap himself for failing to listen to me. So I began settling cases, and if anyone refused to listen the Kiap did put him in jail, and the people saw it was true. The Kiap gave this same kind of job to other men as well.[22] Some of these appointees went off and said, "The white man has turned our stomachs around and put them in again backwards. Don't dare to speak in front of us, we're not in our proper minds, we'll kill you!" If anybody looked boldly at them they said "The kiap has made me a boss boy. Why are you staring at me like that?" The other would reply,

[16] (Name omitted.)

[17] (Names omitted.)

[18] (Ongka does not say, but this was probably a punishment for suspected adultery.)

[19] (George Greathead, in Hagen from 1938 to 1939.)

[20] (Informally appointed officials who assisted government officers prior to the later formal appointment of *luluai* and *tultul*. See L. Mair, *Australia in New Guinea,* London, 1948, p. 53.)

[21] (The apron is thought of as being torn open in the adulterous sexual act. "Tying up the woman's apron" is the traditional Hagen term for compensation for adultery.)

[22] Tipuka Kitepi Rop and Mel and Kawelka Kurupmbo Nikint, for example.

"My sister's son, I wasn't staring at you, I was just looking normally." "No you weren't, you were staring insolently," they said. Then they would take the man and bind him to the central post in a house and build up a fire nearby until he choked in the smoke.[23]

The man would agree then to let go of his pigs as a fine to the boss boy. "I'm dying," they would say. "No you're not, I'm a kiap and I'm watching over you," was the reply, and so they continued until the pigs were promised. When one particular man[24] who was a boss boy went visiting, he would say to the people, "My stomach has turned round, the sun is high in the sky, don't come near me or touch me, I'll kill you!" and all the people fled like pigs into the woods. People used to shake with fear when they saw the boss boys coming with big cassowary plumes nodding on their heads.

I kept quiet about this at the time, then I went and told the kiap later. "What? Who told them to do that?" he said. I was a boss boy for two or three years and then Master Black came.[25] He lived in Nondugl, over to the east, looking after birds and marsupials.[26] I wonder where he is now? He called me in and said that there were several good reports about my work in his office, and he gave me a round badge of office as a *tultul*. I was one of the first to receive these badges, and he told me I was to be the only tultul for six tribes around, and these should all bring their cases of disputes to me at Mbukl. He would send a policeman to live there, for whom a house should be built, and he would assist me to settle the people's problems. I walked home on foot from the government station over the Minembi hills and set about building a station, and later the policeman Mberem came down and joined me there.

The people from all the clans heard about this and, oh, they brought in bagfuls of food and they brought their troubles to me to settle! We built more houses, for the policeman and his interpreters, for the disputants, for the people I sentenced to jail. We built houses till they stretched far on either side of the Mbukl ridge, and made sweet potato gardens all around to feed the people. The clans of different tribes were always fighting and I wondered how I could make them listen to me and stop. So I forced them to dig a huge hole as "jail work." They dug down further and further and handed the earth up to the surface on bark trays with vine ropes until the vines broke with the weight again and again.[27] I did all this because I thought of how hard a life my father had had, with none of the new tools, and I thought, "We can't go back to the old ways in which we turned round and killed our brothers, we must take up the new way in order to get the new things."

---

[23] (Hagen men's houses are round with a strong center post, in front of which a fireplace is maintained.)

[24] (Name omitted.)

[25] (John Black, a patrol officer who went with Taylor on the Hagen-Sepik patrol in 1938. In 1972 he was living in retirement in Australia.)

[26] (More likely he was, as a government kiap, stationed near to the Hallstrom Livestock and Fauna Trust, which was established in 1948 by Sir Edward Hallstrom. If Ongka is referring to this, it would date his appointment as a tultul to the period immediately after the Second World War. On Nondugl see C. Simpson, *Adam in Plumes,* London, 1955, pp. 168 ff.)

[27] (Signs of this very large hole were still visible in 1964.)

Ongka as a Local Government Councillor in 1970 (picture by Sandy Lawson).

So gradually people began to give up fighting. Black changed the policeman a number of times, put in medical orderlies, and after about two years he trusted that we really had a station there, and he distributed tultul badges to about seventeen further men[28] of different groups. To me alone he gave a *luluai's* badge, the long one, and told me that if the tultul had any difficulty in settling cases they should bring them to me, and if I made a decision and it was still not accepted I should bring it to him. In such a case it would not be settled by means of compensation or exchanges; the offender would certainly go to jail in Hagen. One man[29] refused to make returns for a pig he had stolen, saying he was owed it as a compensation payment. I sent him to Hagen. How could he get out? He was so hungry in jail that he had to eat green tobacco leaves until he vomited. The people were startled, they jumped like snails recoiling into their shells. After this, cases which I heard were over promptly. I said I would not listen to lengthy discussions, and people remembered how I had made a man eat green tobacco leaves, so they took me seriously.

After my time as a luluai this business of the local government council came.[30] I had been a boss boy, a tultul, and a luluai, and now I wanted them to give this Council badge only to younger men, but after a while they insisted on giving it to me. I saw how some of the Councilors were sitting on their chairs at meetings and boasting without doing any work, taking their pay for nothing. I was cross with them and told them off, saying that white men who came from the other side of the earth had got here and earned their money by doing difficult jobs, why were the councilors boasting and showing off? I felt this all the time that I was a councilor, and in the end I got tired of it, and said that my "son," Kont,[31] could be the councilor. So he took hold of the position, and now is it going well or not? I don't know.

---

[28] (Names omitted.)

[29] Klamakae Rumba.

[30] (The council was in this area from 1962 onwards.)

[31] (Kont is actually of a different clan from Ongka within the wider Kawelka tribe, and at the time, 1973, there was some dissension between them. In 1975 Ongka saw himself as having voluntarily bowed out. Elections were held again in 1975 and the councilorship went to yet another candidate.)

2 / Games and Tricks

In the past the only strong thing we had was our stone axes. Another thing was a kind of decorating oil which comes from a long way away in the south.[1] Another was our own indigenous ash salt, which we made up into long or fat bundles. For our clothes we took tree bark and fashioned it into a belt for men, while our women made head-nets and front aprons for us. They also used to beat out bark-cloth, for head coverings and for old people to sleep in. Young people with heat in their skin were able to sleep on the ordinary mats, made of tough pandanus leaves, but the old people would grumble, "This mat's too bumpy for me to lie on." So we would take out our beaters and beat and beat the fibers till they spread out very wide and became just like a blanket. We dried it in the sun and took it to our old people and said, "Here, get inside this and nod your head." We younger people simply spread some banana leaves under the ordinary mats and slept quite happily.

Let me go back a bit now to my childhood again. One of the games I played was in the mud, *ui mbrau.* I dug my heels into the mud and traced out a men's ceremonial house. Then I rolled up balls of mud in leaves. I said, "My sow's been served by the boar and it's going to have piglets." Then I lifted up the balls and flung them down so that they burst and mud flew in all directions. "Now my sow's farrowed, let me see how many we've got," I said, and counted the number of little balls again. "With these two I'll get a wife, with these two I'll make exchanges, and these two I'll cook and eat myself," I said, pretending. Another boy would say, "Mine's farrowed too, but the piglets died." Then we would consider why and would say, "I heard a bat squeaking, perhaps that was a bad omen from a ghost. Shall we try divination?" Then we made a special kind of divination with an arrow (in this an expert thrusts a stick or arrow through the wall or into the floor of the house and asks ghosts to take hold of the arrow in response to questions put to them]. One of us took the part of the expert and cured the pig, then finally we would cook and eat it. It was all done with mud, of course, and after some months I grew tired of playing this game.[2]

---

[1] (From Lake Kubutu, via Mendi in the Southern Highlands Province. It is carried in long bamboo tubes. The oil is used to decorate the body for dancing, and whole tubes are given away on ceremonial occasions to exchange partners.)

[2] Other games we had were as follows: in *rua nde,* we placed a banana trunk on a slope and slid down it; in *til roklarorong,* we slid down slopes on leaves; in *mong mal,* we threw pit-pit (cane-grass) stalks at each other; in *renggeip mal,* we played at pushing and shoving; and in *nu-pönt,* we dammed up streams with sticks and mud until the water built up, then we let it break through and sweep down.

We started finding little rats. When one of us made a catch, we set up a shout of delight, and all of us rushed round gathering leaves and greens to cook along with it and wood for the fire. Little girls put the greens in their netbags, and some of them carried cooking stones too, and so we went off, with mighty preparations to cook our tiny prey. We might carry it around till it stank, and then we'd cook it, saying, "This is our male pig we're slaughtering and singeing now." We did everything as if it was a real pig, dividing it into head, legs, and body, and giving the guts and stomach to girls to go and wash. Sometimes a young man would come and discover us and ask us what we were doing, and we would hang our heads and say "Nothing much, it's just a rat we're cooking in the little *wara* spirit house."[3] If he was a good type, he would say, "That's all right, carry on," and leave us to it, but if he was nasty and interfering he would say, "Ah! Open it up quickly and let me see!" We would protest that it was not ready for opening up yet, but he would threaten us until a few of us went over and reluctantly uncovered our little treasure of head, legs, and body in the oven. Then he would snatch it from us, and be off, leaving us to cry and eat up only the greens instead of the meat. We would run home to our fathers and told them how the big boy had come and stolen from us, and we pleaded with them to do something about it. "All right," one of our fathers said, and he quietly walked over to the boy's house. If he found him in, he told him, "You stole from their little oven, didn't you? Had they taken your piglet to cook there?" He beat the boy with a stick and a big fight would break out. After that we felt better and were happy with our father and went off to play somewhere else.

As we grew bigger and went into the forests we might be lucky enough to kill a *kumbaem* or *pil* marsupial, and we were delighted with our achievement. We would make really fine preparations to cook them, cutting wood and banana leaves and butchering them with much care. You can see how we started out, when we were scarcely weaned from the breast, by making little pigs out of mud, then we went on to rats, caught at the edges of gardens, and then we came on to real marsupials.

I had eight special friends from my own clan and two others from the Tipuka, and there were five girls also who went around with us.[4] The boys among us all shared a single men's house to sleep in. As we grew older, when one of our fathers killed and cooked a pig, one or two of us would go and beg for a piece of tongue or some spare ribs or bits of meat. We would plead and plead for a little bit of meat to go and cook in our *wara* oven. Meanwhile we had already told the other boys to prepare wood and leaves and greens at the cooking place. At first our fathers would not listen and said no, but we asked them again and again, saying, "Father, just a little piece please," until one of them cut off a bit and gave it to us. We stuffed it into a netbag filled with parsley and other things begged from our mothers and raced over to where the others were waiting, carrying a glowing firestick with us as a sign of our success, and singing and whistling to let them know

---

[3] (A children's version of spirit houses used for sacrifices in the adult culture.)
[4] (Names omitted.)

we were on the way. When we arrived they were pleased and congratulated us: "Oh, brother, that's wonderful!" They said, "You just stay still and we'll do all the work, you're a big-man!" Quickly they brought up the materials for the oven and heated the stones; their necks were dry with the thought of food. Then we watched the smoke carefully. If it went straight up in the air, we were pleased and said it was a good omen, we would eat pork again soon; but if it spread out and didn't rise, we were disappointed and said it was a bad sign. When we had cooked and removed the food we played at handing it out formally to different "houses" in packages as we saw the elders do. When we'd finished that, we actually mixed it all up again and ate it ourselves together.

These friends of mine were from outside my immediate family. In the family I had some elder sisters. The eldest was Kimbit; she died in childbirth when the placenta would not come out. Then there was Rambe; she was married to a Tipuka Oklembo man, Mel, and had a son, Ken.[5] Then there was myself, then my sister Kokl, who is married to Tipuka Kendike Mel.[6] Kimbit, the first daughter my father had, died before I was old enough to know her and cry for her. My father married one wife from inside the Kawelka tribe, from its other section, the Kundmbo, and another from the Römndi group. By the Römndi wife he had only Nöni, my brother, who is now dead. From my father's brothers there is old Pundukl, son of Öruma, and by Pena there is that son of his,[7] who goes around like a senseless young man in town.[8] Then by Kilwa there is Tiki, who helps me with my work.

My mother, as I say, came from a different section of the Kawelka. Then, as now, the two sections had different territories, and my mother went off to live at her own place, leaving me to stay with my father. There she died when I was still quite young. Sometimes she used to take me up there, although my father opposed it. To protect me, she used to refer to me as her little daughter Kungndi. "Kungndi, come here and put on your girl's apron," she would say, and whenever we went to a funeral or some other public occasion, they looked at me and thought I was a girl. Then once they saw me lift up my apron and urinate and they cried out, "Hey, it's a boy!" Oh, she gathered me up and fled with me like a runaway pig back to Mbukl! The men up there[9] said, "We could have killed him, it was a boy after all!" In those days they let girls be, but boys of enemy groups were killed, for they would later turn into warriors and kill their enemies. So my mother tricked them and that was how I survived.

---

[5] (Ken often comes to Mbukl to stay with and give support to Ongka, his mother's brother.)

[6] (A favorite exchange partner of Ongka's. The sister, he says, is particularly generous to him.)

[7] (Name omitted.)

[8] (This son was a migrant for many years in Moresby, gave up wives his seniors had helped to obtain, and brought danger to Ongka in 1974 over a payback killing issue. In late 1975 he returned home to Hagen.)

[9] (At times, the two sections of Kawelka were fighting with each other. The Kundmbo, where Ongka's mother came from, also had many connections with the other Kawelka's traditional enemies among the Minembi.)

After that I always still wanted to join my mother up at her place, but my father said I would be killed and forbade me. We argued backwards and forwards about it and then I agreed to stay. My mother came back to see me sometimes, till she died. At that time a very bad epidemic of sickness broke out, and people died in large numbers. Some died out in the fields and lay there to rot, others died in their houses and pigs came to eat the corpses, for there was no one to bury them. We had bad running sores on our legs and blood in our excrement. It was a bad time and my mother died then. I was old enough to cry for her. She had recently come to see us and brought me an apron to wear and a present of food. She and her own mother both died at the same time. I was with her and said, "Mother, why are you going to die? Please don't die!" But she died all the same, and so we accepted this. I and my two sisters, Kokl and Rambe, who were growing girls at the time, we set to and made our own gardens, dug our own food, and lived with our father. Then Rambe got married and I stayed with Kokl. I married first, then later she married Mel.

We lived only at Mbukl, we never went to Kuk,[10] which our men had left a long time before. In between were the lands of the Minembi, Kombukla, and Kimke groups, who were all ready to kill us. We thought about it as our forefathers' land, but we could not safely reoccupy it. We sometimes traveled up there quickly with my father, and he pointed out our old settlement places in the abandoned and empty space, and we went back. Usually we would not wander far from our own woods and streams around Mbukl, and as we boys walked around we might see smoke from a fire where one of our fathers was sacrificing a pig at a cemetery or other cult-place. When we saw that, we secretly filed off through the bush and crept up to the spot where they were cooking the pig. From behind the leaves we watched them remove the pork from the oven, divide it out, and eat, and when they had gone we rushed out and gobbled up all the charred greens, bits of bananas that had stuck to the cooking stones, and fragments of bone. We fell on it all like dogs and swallowed it down.

Once we went to watch them cooking pigs down in a hollow. We crept up on the bank above and looked down. The men took a long time about it, and one of us crawled forward and peeped over the edge to see how they were getting on, supporting himself by a creeper tied to a tree trunk. One time, as he balanced himself on the edge, the creeper broke and he tumbled down in a heap among them, landing in the charcoal from the fire they used to heat the cooking stones. He rolled himself into a ball and hid his head in his hands out of shame. They pushed him and turned him over with their feet but he kept silent. One of the men, Ndoa, gave him a kick and asked him, "What have you come for?" Ndoa looked up at the bank and saw marks of our feet on the ground and said, "They came here as a trick, waiting for us to cook and eat the pig and then they would come out and steal the bits." He hauled us out and gave us all kicks. But Kakl, who was a kindly

---

[10] (This is one of the original territories of the Kawelka group, from which they were driven out in warfare before Ongka's birth. Since pacification post-1945 numerous Kawelka men have gone back to resettle the Kuk area, and Ongka himself has a settlement there, where he keeps gardens and two of his wives.)

man, said, "Don't do that, they're only poor boys," and he dusted us down and rubbed pork-fat on our skins. When he divided the pig, he gave us each some to eat for ourselves and some also to take home with us, including pieces of fat and greens. We were delighted with him and made off saying what a good man he was and how bad Ndoa was: "You bad man, you nearly kicked us to death, why did you have to do that?" Of course, we were only young then. Recalling it when I was older, I was very ashamed about it all, but when I was young I didn't realize and did these things anyway.

We were always after pork. Sometimes we would hear of a pig-cooking and secretly followed the people carrying the pork back to their house. We went round the back and made a little hole big enough to get the pork and pass it out to our friends, and we hurried away to the bushes with it. This was outright stealing, it was bad, but we used to do it. The house-owners thought it was a spirit that had eaten the pork, and might try divination procedures to discover why it had happened, whereas all the time it was really we ourselves who did it.

Many people were afraid of ghosts. Adults told us not to go into cemeteries where the ghosts were, for they were dangerous and might attack. When someone had recently died, they told us to get inside the house earlier than usual. We used to come home then before sundown, thinking that otherwise the dead person's ghost standing outside would catch us in its embrace. Sometimes we were told to look after pigs, but if we heard any whistling in the evening we got inside at once, covered up our heads with dry banana leaves, and slept; meanwhile, thieves outside would steal the pigs.

This kind of thing could happen when our older kin went off to a pig-killing for a marriage or a sacrifice or a moka gift,[11] leaving us small children behind. Thieves would come up and hoot and whistle like ghosts: "Who-o-o are you people here? Go-o-o inside the house, go inside!" We rushed in and buried ourselves in leaves and rags. "Get your heads down and keep them down, or the spirits will take you off to their place!" the thieves said. Then they came right inside the house and took the belongings, netbags and grease-flasks, all covered with soot from the fires, arrows, stone axes, pigs, whatever was available. They took them away and how could you find them again? Not a hope. Later the owners would say it was spirits who had done it; of course it was only a bunch of tricks played by thieves, but people thought it was true, and meanwhile the thieves got away with the goods.

Another time thieves wanted to steal his only pig from Nöni, an old bachelor. He used to tie it to a stake by its rope and leave it to forage in the dirt for grubs in a grassy patch of bushland. The thieves decorated up a man, painting his whole body with red, white, blue, and charcoal stripes, putting a gourd mask over his face, and painting his eyes all white. Then they all waited in the bush, holding on to the pig by its rope. The poor man came up to collect his pig and found that the rope was tight and led into the undergrowth. He followed it to see

---

[11] (The chief kind of ceremonial gift-giving in Mount Hagen society. See introduction and A.J. Strathern, *The Rope of Moka,* Cambridge, 1971.)

what had happened. The decorated man was waiting. He had tied down his nose
with a thong, so that his voice came out all nasalized: "I've given all my land to
you, and yet you come here digging, digging, digging at it again. Who are you?"
he said, impersonating a bush spirit, and he charged out and seized the old man's
hair. Poor Nöni dropped the pig rope and fled. The "spirit" gave chase, he fled, it
chased him, he fled, it chased him. They raced and raced together until Nöni leapt
across a stream and left the spirit behind. The spirit then returned to the pig and
he and his two accomplices collected it. Nöni was convinced it really was a spirit
that had attacked him: "It nearly killed me! It bit me and bit me and drove me
home!" he said. Next day he and others went back to the scene of the theft and
there on the ground were the discarded mask and thong which the thief had used
in his disguise. "Oh! You were fooled by a thief!" they said. These were the kinds
of tricks I saw people play when I was a boy.

In those days both adults and children were full of tricks. If a man wanted to
steal something he would announce to people that he was sick and going to die.
He would stay in his house and refuse food for two whole days, saying to visitors,
"I'm dying, Go and cut some firewood please and look after things for me, could
you?" They believed him and went off. While they were away he got up and raced
round, stealing pigs, netbags, grease-flasks, cassowaries, all kinds of things which
he left hurriedly with helpers, then returned home to lie on his sickbed. If anyone
suspected him, others would counter, "What, him? No, he's been sick in bed for
several days. We're wondering if he's going to die. It couldn't be him." But it was.
A similar trick was to say one was going on a long journey to the Jimi Valley and
to be seen walking over the hills in that direction. Then the "traveler" would dou-
ble back and steal a pig, while people said, "We saw him all decorated up on his
way to the Jimi. It must have been someone else."

Children played tricks too. If a child was lost, we would say that perhaps a
spirit had taken it and swallowed it whole; and children themselves made up stories like this. If they were left behind somewhere and wandered off by themselves,
when they came back they were afraid their parents would be cross with them, so
they said, "An old man came and took me away and I slept at his place in the
cemetery." The parents heard this and said, "Oh, a ghost must have come to take
the soul of the child away to the cemetery. Now we must cook a small pig and tie
a strong vine to the child's thumb in order to get the soul back." One of the senior
men in our small group, Kandekl, used to make the spells for this. He took leaves
of the *kuklumb* plant (which we also use in some of our rituals to get wealth) and
brushed them against the vine, blowing a spell onto it to make the child's spirit
travel back along the vine and reenter his body. Once Kandekl did this for a boy
called Tip, the son of old Kakl, and when it was over the boy revealed it was all a
trick he had invented as an excuse to avoid getting into trouble for not cutting
firewood as he had been told. The men were so angry they took bunches of leaves
and beat him for this.

Another thing I did as a boy was to hunt for frogs, which left their spawn on
swampy stretches of land where cane-grass grew. We would light blazing torches
at night, and follow up to the heads of streams, following, following, following,
up the big Möka river to the heads of the mountains. We carried many torches

with us and gathered the frogs in bundles, putting them into small netbags.[12] It would be daylight when we returned with our load, and we cut firewood and leaves and cooked the frogs, putting layers of hot stones alternately with frogs in the oven. Then we spat our own salt and ginger root over them; they were delicious, very sweet!

These were the only kinds of treats we had. What other foods were there? There were none. Warfare was all around us; how could you travel and get special foods? We were afraid to go even a mile or two away, so we stayed in our own places and never went elsewhere. That was why we had to collect frogs, birds, marsupials, and grubs from our own clan areas, or, when there were none of these to be caught, we were reduced to searching for little rats among the leaves of sweet potato plants. Those of us who were near the forest trees searched these for grubs; those who lived by streams looked for the little fish. They propped these on sticks, piercing them through their gills, for frying, and men laid them into banana leaves and made long sausages of them, picking out the backbones before eating them.

When we wanted to go courting it was difficult to get good decorations. We used to gather seeds of the *ndulkina* plant and make necklaces of these. We wore marsupial teeth and tails and snail shells. We caught a small parrotlike bird in the holes of trees and used its feathers, which were nice and bright. We searched for sprigs of green forest plants such as the low-growing *mul tei* and for big white *mara*[13] leaves, and for a kind of bamboo shoot, which we shaped up and incised for wear as a forehead ornament. We used to share small lumps of pig-fat with which to rub our skin. There was not much and we shared it out: "Brother, use mine now; yesterday we used yours." We visited one another's houses at night to sleep and shared also a little sugarcane or bananas before sleeping. Next day we went to a different house, and so on. Thinking of how we would be hungry later, we planted up gardens for each one of our group, and when we had finished one job we moved on to the next.

When our work in the gardens was finished, we used to go out courting. Sometimes we went northwards over into the Jimi Valley or even ventured eastwards among the Tipuka clans. We decorated ourselves slowly and carefully, then we went out and walked around and around, coming back only at dawn. Every day we shifted to a new place, until our parents became angry and said, "Looking for women, are you, and running about day after day after day?" They took sticks and beat us and gave us a real telling-off, and we would run away to another house. The same thing would happen there, and so we carried on until eventually we married and settled down. Then each one of us built his own house, and we realized what wild madcaps we'd been before. Later, when the administration came, we quieted down further again. After we were married, we thought that if we gadded about too much our wife's brothers our father would come and say, "Doesn't your husband do any work, then? Doesn't he build a house and look

---

[12] Some of the kinds we caught were *kuklma, nde rok, kilönamb, pekerep,* and *pokapokl.*
[13] *(Lauraceae cryptocarya.)*

after you?" If they were to say that, we would be very ashamed, we realized, and so we stopped chasing around and got down to some work.

In those days, as I have said, we used to pay for wives with stone axes. The small kind, which we used for cutting little trees and chopping branches, we lined up in sets of ten. Big ones like *tinggrina, nggaema, ketepukla,* they might give anything from one to eight of these, all carefully bound and displayed. Long spears were laid down in lines and the axes placed in rows within these. They pushed the ax handles into the ground, and as men stood in a row watching, the giver walked down the line calling out the names of the types of ax, *ketepukla, tinggrina nggömbil, tinggrina pokan, yambina, mbukl maemb, kuntin, nggaema,* and so on. At the end of the row he said, "With these I strike the head of the bride and take her." If he perhaps had a single pearl shell and one or two sets of cowrie shells strung into ropes, he would give these also, but otherwise just the axes.

Special axes were hung in a netbag and given to the bride's close kin; the smaller ones were lined up and divided out to the less closely related kin. Some of these too were for goods to be presented back by the girl's side. Shells they hung on some of the axes and gave to the close kin also. The bride's people sent some axes back to enable the husband to work and support his wife. Some pigs might be given too, but the axes were the essential thing; if axes were not given they would refuse the marriage, saying, "He's a rubbish, useless man, what shall we do? Don't let's give him the girl."

3 / Where Are You, Boys?

When I was a boy I played around in the woods all day and at night went home. My parents had told me to look after the pigs and watch they did not stray, and when I forgot this and went off to play instead, they said to themselves, "I wonder if he'll come back hungry for his supper tonight? Perhaps we'll see him then." After it was dark I would come back, and, afraid that they would be cross with me, I stood outside and scratched at the door and walls of our house, listening to them talking inside, my mother busy making a netbag. She heard me scratching outside and said, "There are some rats creeping around the back of the house! Where do they think they're going?" I and the other children waited again for a while, and then the parents said, "Ah, our children! We told them to look after the pigs and instead they went off to the woods and streams to make mudpies and slides for themselves. So they've come home and want to get inside the house, do they? Where will they go? I'll kill them. I'll beat them with nettles and sticks. Eating mushrooms all day instead of looking after the toddlers and fixing up the pigs' ropes! So now they come and want some food, do they?" We thought, "Oh! If we go in they'll really kill us!" and so we stayed out all night, hanging around in the long cane-grass, heads bowed down with the cold but sticking it out until morning came. When the sun rose and our numb skin was warmed a little we went into houses nearby and found hot sticks that had been pushed into the ashes of fireplaces. These we took and went to the edges of gardens where we pulled off shoots and greens, anything we could find, and cooked these on improvised fires built out of small fragments of wood. We might also steal some sweet potatoes and *pit-pit*,[1] and surreptitiously run off into the bush, saying, "Now they'll really beat us if they find us."

Thinking of this, we searched for a place that was really dry and free of puddles and made a hut for ourselves, planting cane sticks first as walls and then sticking branches into the ground and bending them over to form a kind of canopy. On top of this again we piled up leaves and sticks until it was enough. With the hut complete, we ran back to the gardens to steal more small sweet potatoes and bananas, pushing these into the tops of our bark belts so as to conceal them. We cooked these in our hideout, leaving a little pile for the next day, and when it grew dark we crawled carefully on all fours into the hut, as a pig does into its nest, and once inside we put our heads down and slept. Our skin was numb with cold, and grasshoppers and other creepy-crawlies would come and bite us, waking us up with a start, then we would try to snuggle down again. Pigs are used

[1] (*Setaria palmaefolia,* sometimes known as New Guinea asparagus.)

to sleeping outside but people are not! We might have died of it, but we didn't; maybe our ancestral ghosts were watching and helped us. At night if rain came it got in everywhere. We had to cover our faces in our hands and bear it, until our cold skins were like a squelchy sodden stick one treads underfoot. But we slept on and on until at dawn the first birds cried out and we would wake up, our legs and arms all stiff; how could we manage to stand up and go outside?

Often there was an early mist and drizzle, but when the sun came through we crawled out and dragged ourselves to a sunny spot beside a garden or a little knoll, and there we lay and lay until the warm sun ate into our bones and eventually we were strong again. We waited until we thought that people would have gone off to work, then hungry and tired we slowly made our way in the direction of the houses. We crept into the houseyards, removed the boards from the doorway, and took out kindling for fire. We slunk alongside gardens again, popping up and down and weaving in and out to see if people were watching. With our teeth we tore the bark from pieces of wood to make them into digging sticks and with these we made little jabs at the sweet potato patches to secure a few tubers which we carefully lined in our belts again. When our belts were full we hopped over the fence, taking care to avoid being seen, and disappeared into the undergrowth with our loot. We went some distance before we made a fire, thinking that it would be seen and they would follow our footsteps, catch us, and beat us, so we went right into the woods, and there we set up little fires and cooked our food. We liked the sweet potatoes best for they made us feel full; if it was only bananas or sugarcane we quickly felt hungry again. If there were any to spare we put them aside for later.

Meanwhile our parents thought, "We told them off and they ran away. If they stay out too long they'll go crazy." So they began to search and call out for us. Maybe our mother or our father would be sorry for us and come calling, "Where are you, boys?" We answered, and he would come and take hold of us. Then he would say, "If you stay out here, a tree will fall on you, a snake will bite you, or a spirit will get you. Spirits make houses like pig nests for themselves out here and one will drag you off. It will box your ears so you can't hear or think properly, then take you to the cemetery place and gobble you down, bones and all. Or if it doesn't, you'll be washed away by a river or freeze to death in the rain. Pigs, birds, and marsupials live outside, but people don't; they go inside their houses, build a fire, and keep themselves warm. Now come and stay with us or you'll go crazy and die." They spoke like that to make us afraid, and so we listened to them and went home.

This time we would split sticks for the fire, fill up bamboos of water, and look after other people's children nicely without hitting them. When the adults came we quickly told them, "I've cut wood, filled up water, seen your child doesn't crawl into the fire and looked after it nicely." So they said, "Oh, what a kind boy! Well, I've dug out some nice big sweet potatoes, just for you!" They gave us good greens, bananas, and *pit-pit* for being so well behaved, and said how pleased they were and that we should carry on in the same way. If we afterwards went back to our old wild ways, they grew really cross and beat us.

In those days if people left their houses they always had to leave someone on guard against thieves, and they warned us not to be fooled by strange whistlings into thinking that it was spirits who were coming, but to stick together and watch over the pigs and not to forget and run off to the stream to drink water. If they had gone to a bride-wealth payment or a pig kill, we used to cut bundles of wood and place them in the front yard and stack bamboo tubes of water in the cool shade of a tree, and when they came back we ran out and pointed to all this. So again they praised us—"Oh! Oh! You've done well"—and they gave us steamed food or sugarcane and we ate and were happy. Day after day we looked after the house in this way, until they said, "You're probably tired of staying at home all the time, this time come with us." At a bride-wealth we would be invited along with other families to eat some of the cooked pork which was presented. The people who were cooking reckoned up the numbers of legs of pork they had available for different people, then made their invitation. If we were invited, they told me to wash, rub pig-grease on my skin, put on a new front apron and rear covering of cordyline leaves, and come along to share in the pork. When our people got their pork, the man dividing it up would give me a piece with a bone or a foot along with it and say, "This is for the one who looks after the house so well." I was delighted and grateful. Later I had a share too in the main piece of pork after they brought it home and recooked it.

Another day I would grow tired of the house and I would go and join the adults in their work. They might be carrying logs to make fences or lopping branches from trees that were to stand and become dry in the gardens, and I would come up and carry a log or two or pick up a handy ax and lop a branch, and they would encourage me, saying, "That's right, that's right! Look, he's lopping the branches!" So I thought, "That's how one works. Now if only I could make a little garden of my own and my fathers and brothers could come in and help me as I help them. That would be good." I asked my father and told him if he would just fell the big trees from an area I would tackle the undergrowth, and he said, "What? Oh yes, that's good. You can try it out on a small area and if you do well you can go on to make a bigger garden later. I'll do the edges and fences for you; you do the middle bit." So I went at it with flailing stick-knife[2] in the heat of the sun, eager to make the garden. My father was pleased. I tried to cut the fence stakes myself too, but my stone ax was not sharp and kept glancing off the wood. It was hard work! My father sharpened the ax for me and straightened out some of the stakes which I had hacked at. He taught me how to cut down trees, split them into sections, fashion the stakes and strengthen the fence after the uprights were in place. Sometimes I laid the stakes horizontally and lashed them to uprights on either side. My father told me to use two lengths of lashing at a time for strength instead of just one. When the fence was at last finished I waited for a good dry day, then burnt off the undergrowth. Then we made the drainage trenches in it to carry off rainwater, and divided out the sections to different people for the actual planting. In one part I

[2] (A sharpened stick used to cut undergrowth.)

planted bananas and sugarcane, and below that taro, parsley, *pit-pit,* and *keng-gopa.*[3] Actually the men planted sugarcane first, then long *pit-pit,*[4] then bananas and various greens. The women planted taro, yams, short pit-pit, kinds of greens, beans, and wing-beans. Then we watched while the first shoots came through and people said, "This is the first time he's put his hand to garden making." My father said, "Yes, so don't take the greens and the cucumbers from the garden yet. First let us go into the forest to cook a marsupial which we can eat with the greens." He was in fact thinking of using a young pig as a sacrifice, if we couldn't find any marsupials. My father told the women to fetch the first harvest of greens. My father led a piglet out to the spirit house where we used to sacrifice to the ghosts, and he made a prayer: "My boy has never made a garden before, this is his first attempt, so in future may all his work be successful":

Let the greens be sweet,
Let the sweet potatoes swell and be fat,
Let the taro shoots grow,
Let the bananas ripen in big bunches,
Let the sugarcane grow tall and straight,
Let the long pit-pit be heavy in its sheath,
Let all the food be good and none fail.
This is his first garden.
I cook a pig for him and
Draw the garden into cultivation from the bush.
Let none of the food crops fail.

Afterwards, of course, I planted many gardens with no ceremony; this was just for my first effort.[5] Later, if we hunted and found some marsupials, we might cook them for the ghosts also and tell them, "This is a present for his first garden, later he won't give you any presents, this is just for his first one."

I made this garden before I was really grown up. The grease had not really come into my face. Later, when I put on the full bark-belt and apron of a man, I went foraging in the deep woods. When I was hungry I set marsupial traps. I shaped up a long log of wood and carried it to the bush, where I set it up as a deadfall, suspended from vines and baited with a piece of sweet potato. I chewed some sweet potato, then spat pieces all around so that the marsupials would come in, smell it and nibble at the bait; then the log would fall and crush the animal. I set up dozens of traps like this up and down the streamsides, pointing this way and that, and left them overnight. At dawn I checked them out, moving all the way upstream on one side and downstream on the other, resetting the traps in which an animal had been taken. I gathered my catch and gutted the animals at the stream one by one. I wiped the insides with ferns, removed the excrement, separated the livers from the rest of the entrails, and made little

---

[3] *(Rungia klosii.)*
[4] *(Saccharum edule.)*
[5] Nowadays we speak of rituals like this as *kela memb,* a "blessing," as the missionaries say, but before we used to refer to this as *kukilimb mondoromen,* "they push back the undergrowth."

heaps of them. The short and fat ones I used to call "nongopas,"[6] and the long thin ones I called "stringies."

As the sun rose up I carried the carcasses along with a kindling of wood along the pathway to the *wara* spirit house, collecting parsley and other greens on the way. There I dug out the earth oven, and collected leaves of the *röu* and cordyline plants for the cooking. I piled up the cooking stones, chopped wood neatly for the fire, singed and scraped the carcasses twice over. The bad scrapings I threw away, but the bits where the animal's fur smells sweet I scraped onto the greens to flavor them. I cooked them in the oven, laid out carefully so that when it was opened people could count how many there were. Then I rushed off to tell my father and the others, knowing that dogs and pigs might come to disturb the oven. I told them, "I checked my trap this morning. I didn't catch any, just one little rat. Would you like to come and share it with me?" "All right" they said, and came. I had sprinkled the bodies all over with a mixture of ginger and our own ash salt, and when they tasted them they said, "Oh! You've really cooked them well, they're delicious!" So that encouraged me to set up my traps again and sometimes I might get a really big marsupial in them.

Over to the southwest, on the slopes of Mount Hagen itself, they catch marsupials in another way, called *kui kilimb ou.* A man constructs a long fence by joining pieces of wood together, as a baffle for the marsupials, in places setting a loop for them and constructing a small ramp up to it. The baffle stretches all the way up a hill, and the animals look for a way to get over it, climb the ramps and are noosed. The hunters collect them, gut them, and place them on trestles inside their houses. Making several separate catches, they pile them up for two or three weeks perhaps, until the original ones caught are stiff and encrusted with smoke from the fire. Then they carry them out with care to a pool of clean, shallow water where they lay down ferns and immerse the brittle bodies for softening and washing. They remove the dust and smoke, and the bodies swell and are clean again. Then they wrap them round and round with greens and cook them in the steam-ovens; dividing them out to all their families, they finally enjoy the results of their hunting. This is called cooking *kui makl.*[7]

In the past we used to make these special efforts to get treats of food for ourselves. Over in the valley areas to the east where there aren't any marsupials people used to catch dozens of little fish, *oma tilik,* spit them on sticks and bring them home for steam-cooking. People caught little rats, *kui kuimbuk,* in grassland areas too. Boys found the runways of these little creatures by poking underneath the grass covers. Then they told others to beat the bushes further up the hillside. The rats ran down in confusion and were seized by the tail and stunned. Dozens and dozens might be taken in this way. Women, too, who were walking by streams and felt hungry would catch little tadpoles for themselves, wrap them in leaves, and cook them, along with the small forest frogs which taste fresh and sweet.

---

[6] This was from a man called Nongopa, who had a big stubby penis.

[7] Up in the really high forests hunters may preserve the carcasses of animals by binding them with leaves and placing them in cool shady spots, but not for so long as with *kui makl.*

4 / My First Wife

When we courted girls, if a girl wanted to marry a particular boy, she kept him going with the courting songs all night until it was dawn. Then, as he went outside, she would chase him and plaster his head with ashes, rubbing it right into his skin on all sides. She and her mother and other kin would cover him with mud, all over his apron, his feather headdress, his marsupial furs, everything. They pushed him over and trod him into the dirt, till eventually he got away and made off to a place where he could wash himself. While he was about this, the other boys would come up and tell him to return now to the girl's place, for her parents had said, "We hit him and covered him with mud and ashes. Now bring him back to us and we'll rub grease into his skin and decorate him." So he returned and they decorated him, painting his face, and they sent their daughter back with him to receive courtesy gifts known as *keka* from his people. They had expected this and had cut wood and steam-cooked food for him and his girl, who came to sleep the night at his place along with smaller girl-companions. Next morning they were given presents: marsupial fur to wear in the ears, cassowary quills to slot through their noses, necklaces made from vines and seeds, and incised bamboos to be worn in armlets.

Sometimes the boy would actually marry the girl to whom he gave *keka,* but sometimes she would go off and marry someone else. Then the first boyfriend would go to her house and burn a fire in front of it. If they were nasty people, her parents might take sticks and beat him for this, but if they were good people who behaved properly, they would be sorry for him and say that he was her friend who gave her *keka.* They would say, "Let us break off a piece of pork and give it to him," and so they did and he was happy. If they were unpleasant folk, they would tell him there was none to spare and drive him off. He would go away in a huff and would pick a fight with them on some later occasion, remembering their refusal.

When I was courting, some of the girls wanted to marry me and told me so, but my father said, "Wait, you'll want to marry every one of them, but some of them have no sense in their heads. Let me see them all first and then choose one for you. If you look at them, you'll be taken by the ones with big breasts and fine big arms and legs. Never mind all that. I'll look out for a girl for you. It doesn't matter if she's small or plain in the face; all that matters is her two hands. I'll find out how she makes gardens and tends pigs. If she doesn't listen to her parents but just thinks of holding up her head and going around courting all the time, she'll be no good. So don't show off by choosing a girl for yourself; I will pick one who is hard-working and obedient." I replied, "Oh, father, don't talk like that. There are girls around here

I've made friends with by singing to them and playing at mud-games with them. I like them and may want to marry one of them." But my father said again, "Don't think I'm talking about their looks. I'm thinking of a girl who can help you in your work so you can support each other and you won't be a rubbish-man but will come to be successful and a big-man." I thought, "What's this about being a big-man? I just want a nice-looking girl." However, I said all right and waited. Four different girls from the Oklembo and Kitepi clans came to me, but none of them suited. My father repeated his idea: "I want to get you a girl who works, one who doesn't chatter and gossip, one who gets her hands dirty and does what she is told, not a fancy one who talks a lot and wears all kinds of decorations."

So, when he had obtained the cowrie shell I spoke of earlier, he obtained for me the Oklembo girl Pau. She brought me many pigs with which to start our herd, and we built a very long house for the pigs as more were bred from the first ones. I kept other men living with me to help me with the work, five or six of them.[1] Up at Pokalpana in the grove of holm-oak trees I built a really long women's house, and beyond this in the forest areas uphill we made some huge extended sweet potato gardens, planting sections of the gardens day by day and pushing the cultivated areas further and further up the hill. My wife was a really strong woman, but the work was too much even for her, and her younger sister, Wora, came to stay with us and help. Later I married her off to Eltimbo Mitipa, and then her father and some of her brothers, driven out in warfare, came to stay with us too. We worked together in the gardens, not stopping even to wash ourselves. Another sister of Pau's, called Ka, came to stay with us too.[2] So, to begin with, I had my wife and her two sisters and then her mother and her father, I had my own father to look after the house yard and keep the fires going at home, and I had four young men of our own group and myself the fifth. In one day the whole company of us could finish a sweet potato or a vegetable garden section. The pigs we reared! We bred more and more litters. The women harvested netbags of sweet potatoes for them, dropped their loads and went out for more.

All this work we did with stone tools only. There were very few of the new axes about. We kept on building extensions to the houses for more pig stalls. With this stock in hand, the first enterprise I took on was to obtain a wife for my brother Nöni. I got him a woman of Palke tribe from the Jimi Valley and paid two sets of eight pigs in bride-wealth for her, and with the pigs that were returned by her kinsfolk I put together another bride-wealth on behalf of another of my helpers, Koepa. I paid out another two sets of eight pigs for him. Then I gave eight pigs to my father-in-law, saying, "Your daughter's two hands have done work for me and reared pigs, this is a payment to you for her hands." Then she bore her first child, my daughter, Raem, and brought her up, and weaned her, and became pregnant again, but this time she fell sick. I wondered why. Did the ghosts feel angry about something or what was it?

---

[1] Nikint, Koepa, Engk, Nöni (who is now dead), Pundukl, and Pena.
[2] By this time the white men were making roads, and we were called over to help make the big road that runs into the Baiyer Valley. We became friendly with the road workers and they asked us to give them a woman, so we gave her to them; she was married to a man who was an overseer on the road work, from Ndika Pangaka clan.

She miscarried. Her sickness became severe. It is only now we have hospitals to go to, there were no hospitals then. The pigs I sacrificed on her behalf, with no success! My father was dead by that time, and I asked his spirit not to "hit" her; I begged my mother's spirit too. Every day I cooked another pig, but all these efforts slid off the surface of the problem, they did not penetrate below to settle it. I sent her back to her own place, with a pig as a gift. It was still no use. I cooked all my pigs, first one set of eight, then another, trying to make her get better, hanging their jawbones on the crooks of trees until they were all finished.

The policeman Mberem, who stayed with me at the Mbukl station, came and said how sorry he was, but what could he or I do? There was no road to Hagen in those days; we were in the big bush and we had no medicines. Mberem was with me when she finally rattled in her throat and died. Oh, the people who came to the funeral! In those days we made no coffins but bound up the corpses in leaves, especially wide banana leaves, then lashed it with vines to a long pole and carried the body down to the cemetery. We used to lower the body into a shallow grave, cut free the lashings and strew leaves over it, then fitted pieces of wood on top of this, and finally packed earth over it all.

In this case, as the husband, I was told to stay away. It was the custom for the husband not to go too close to the grave if a young wife of his died because her ghost would be jealous and come to attack him when he tried to marry his next wife. It would come and scratch at his back, pull at him, give him bad dreams, and kill him. To stop this from happening, ritual experts were called in and they kept the man a little way aside from the main activities. They poured water over him and told him to eat some magical substances along with salt.[3] Later they put him in another house, his skin was oiled, his face painted, and he was told not to live in his old houses but to build new ones, all to keep the ghost from returning, to separate it from the husband and drive it away. So the men told me to follow the custom now or the ghost would kill me, but I wouldn't listen to them. "She was my first wife that my father got for me. I was fond of her and I'm upset that she's dead. I won't listen to that kind of nonsense, so don't speak about it to me!" I said. Mberem said how sorry he was and that he would do something about it. He told the men to prepare a section of tree bark, and he brought out his own sheet which he slept on. He washed the body and clothed it with a dress and blouse belonging to his Chimbu wife, sprinkled talcum powder all over it, wrapped it in the sheet, and over this he placed the blanket he had given me, then folded her in the tree bark. We carried her down and made a grave for her near the entrance to the cemetery, a strong grave supported with struts of wood. This was the first grave made there; after that, others began to bury their dead in the same place and to clean the cemetery.

This way of burying her was just something new which Mberem and I did, but others afterwards followed the new way I had set. Before my wife died she had said to me, "You've cooked so many pigs for me while I'm still alive and you've suffered a lot; now you don't have to cook any more for me to end the

---

[3] These were *nde kraep* bark, the *ndingömbukl* vine, the *eipta* vine, and pandanus leaves, all sharp, thorny things which would prick the ghost if it came.

period of funeral mourning when I am dead. You have no pigs left anyway. I'm your wife, but I'm leaving you with so much work, so many gardens and houses, and our little girl too—who will look after her? No, keep your pigs and get another wife to live and work with you." These were her last words to me, and then she died. So I was determined to do well by her, and I buried her with care and looked after our little orphan daughter.

Nothing went wrong, and after some months had gone by I thought, "I have this little girl to take care of, I think I'd better get another wife." So I prepared a bride-wealth of 20 pigs and through my friendship with the policeman Mberem I had secured ten steel axes. At the occasion of payment men were so excited by these that they fought over them in the distribution. This wife was Ruk. Later, with a fresh set of pigs, I married Kae, my Tipuka Wanyembo wife, and with another set again I married my Kawelka Kundmbo wife, Rumbukl, the mother of my son Namba. Most recently, after the 1974 moka festival was over, I married my Oklembo wife, Mande. So I have continued, following the last words of my first wife, marrying successive wives as time goes on, and making moka exchanges and cooking pigs.

As I progressed in my exchange activities, women would come to me and say, "You're a big-man! Let me marry you." "All right," I said, and married them. But later if I saw them running around with other men, I told them to be off; if there were any children I kept all of them, saying, "You didn't bring these with you when you came as a girl to me," and sent the woman off to marry someone else if she liked. If I had shown I was sad about this, other men would have called me a rubbish-man, so I just sent them back home and didn't think about it again. The woman would say, "Oh, Ongka, why are you driving me out? What about all my things and my children?" This was what I did with one of my wives. She used to tell me, "Ongka, I've been working so hard in the garden," and I thought that was good. But later someone told me she was going with other men, and so I dismissed her, keeping my two daughters. A woman is only a woman; she does not have the strength a man has. If she tries to argue with you, you should be tough and frown. Then what will she do, where will she go? She will come back and say, "I wasn't trying to be cross."

Some of the women who came to me I could not afford to marry at the time. The Oklembo woman Rön came and stayed for a month, but I had no wealth available then, so I told her to go. Another Oklembo woman, Ui, whom I had courted before and liked, came to me too and stayed for months, making gardens for me, from which we ate the cucumbers. I wanted her and tried to use a pig of mine as part of a bride-wealth for her. It was being cared for by a man of the Kitepi clan, Nikint, for me; he had actually given it to me after I gave him some grease of the yellow pandanus fruit.[4] But he refused to let it go for this purpose, saying he would not allow it to be given to enemies of his.[5] So Ui had to leave me. Then there was also Ndau. She was a woman of our own Kawelka tribe. Her sister's

---

[4] (A delicacy collected from friends in the Jimi Valley.)
[5] (The Kitepi and Oklembo are allied clans in the Tipuka tribe, but they did sometimes fight, and perhaps this man had a relative killed in such fighting.)

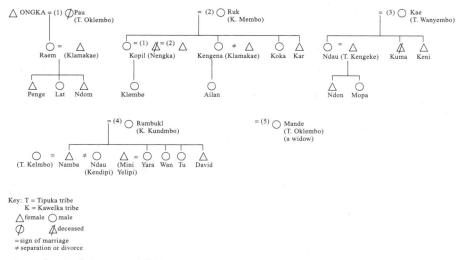

Figure 4.1 *Ongka's wives and children.*

husband, Rokla, a big-man of Oklembo clan, cooked two pigs as a present, and sent them with her for me to marry her. I divided out the pork to everyone in the tribe who helped me with bride-wealth; we took one side for ourselves within the family. Next day, however, the girl slipped away, explaining later that she preferred to marry a previous boyfriend, so I dropped that too. She lives not far from here. Sometimes I give her a lift in my car,[6] saying, "We're real enemies, but have a ride in the car anyway."

About that wife of mine who had intercourse with other men. I brought her before a policeman and put her and the man in court. I took pigs in compensation, and the matter was over. But then she did it again, with men of our own tribe, and of Tipuka and finally with the Minembi, our enemies. So I was tired of it and told her to leave and marry elsewhere. There were dangers for me in this;[7] that was why I put her aside. We used to marry only close by in those days—"outside" women were too dangerous—and even now men tell me not to marry outside women, for if they kill me my group will be left in difficulties.

I have had many children,[8] and if any one of them refuses to listen to what I say, I take them by the hand and throw them out, putting a fence between myself

---

[6] (At the time a Toyota Scout pickup truck, purchased in 1974. Ongka raised money to buy a series of three cars after the mid-1960s: one a Toyota Land Cruiser purchased by the whole tribe in 1965, the second a Nissan truck bought by himself in the late 1960s, and the third, his Toyota Scout.)

[7] (Enemies might seduce her and persuade her either to administer sorcery stuff to Ongka or to bring some part of his personal leavings to them for them to work sorcery on and so to kill their opponent in warfare.)

[8] (See Figure 4.1.)

and them and telling them not to come to my house.[9] Those who do listen to me I look after, and I give them pork, saying, "I do worthwhile things, so if you want to learn from me, come and learn." But if they are headstrong and won't listen, I say, "Don't come near me. You won't listen to what I say, so I won't touch you. You can go around by yourself."

It is the same if a man marries a wife. He gives pigs, axes, cassowaries, everything that is valuable for her, and if she stays by him and has intercourse only with him he is pleased. But if she goes secretly to other men he becomes angry and says, "I gave plenty of wealth for you, don't you know?" Sometimes a husband takes an ax to the wife and splits her head open, killing or at least wounding her. Some men say they don't want to get into trouble; they just divorce the wife and claim back their bride-wealth, since she has made a fool of them. But a strong man says, "Where do you think you'll go to?" and beats the wife or kills her with his ax. A mild man simply says, "That's all right, carry on, but not with me. You can go your own way, and I'll get my bride-wealth back and that will be an end of it."

The parents may become involved. If they don't want their daughter to misbehave like this, they tell her that if she does people will talk behind her back and point their fingers derisively at her. They say the daughter should listen to her husband and work hard for him, and not be lazy or run around talking to other men. If she works well, they say, the husband will be pleased and say to her kinsfolk when they visit, "The wife you sent to me has a good pair of hands," and he will pay the kin for those hands which work so willingly: a valuable shell, a cassowary, a pig, or money. But if she behaves like a flibbertigibbet and doesn't work, the husband will say they gave him a crazy, useless wife. She will have to carry on her mad ways by herself. There will be nothing kept for her either by her husband or her brothers, she will be given no share of any distributions of food and will get herself nowhere.

Fathers tell their sons that if in-laws come they must not frown but must call them by the proper terms[10] and say, "My in-law, you have come. I'm afraid I have no wealth or good food in my house at present, but tell me anyway why you have come." Fathers say to their sons that when in-laws visit they must not go off to play cards[11] or into the forest to hunt, but stay at home and greet the visitors, and if they have some small wealth item to give it to them when they ask for help with a bride-wealth or some other payment. "Then," they say, "they will speak well of you at their own place to the other in-laws, and these will then help you if you

---

[9] (This policy led to some problems of hostility between Ongka and his oldest surviving son, Namba. In Namba's adolescence the two even came to blows at times. Ongka obtained a wife for Namba when he was still in his teens, explicitly to encourage him to build himself a separate house and so differentiate himself from his father. Conflict between them centered most frequently on the use of Ongka's car, which Namba drove for him, skillfully but occasionally in a less than sober state.)

[10] (A son-in-law may not use his father-in-law's or mother-in-law's name; he must call them by the correct in-law term or by the name of their group. He must also not walk behind their backs.)

[11] (The card game Lucky, and other games such as Sweep and Seven, are very popular among people under 40 years of age throughout the Highlands area.)

Ongka's wife Rumbukl and her daughter Yara decorated for a dance in November 1971.

Yara and companion at the dance, November 1971.

Rumbukl at the dance, held at Maninge ceremonial ground. She is a leader in the women's dancing and here takes a brief rest.

Rumbukl and companion lead a group of female dancers, beating hour-glass drums.

1974. Ongka's son by Rumbukl, Namba (in centre) dances with other schoolboys at a celebration for Papua New Guinea's Self-Government (prior to Independence in 1975). The boys are holding the country's national flag, and Namba has borrowed Ongka's gold-colored chain.

are in need or trouble and will say of you that you are a good man who respects his in-laws."

In the case of the wife again, if she doesn't look after her husband but clears off and leaves him to his own devices and won't listen to his talk, he says, "All right." But when her kin come to see him he thinks, "She doesn't look after me, she doesn't give me food, she doesn't care for my pigs, so who are these people, I don't know them." He goes off. Her parents are surprised and say, "Where's your husband? Don't you and he sit down and talk to each other?" She is embarrassed and says, "Yes, we do. I wonder where he's gone." But other people around tell the parents, "She doesn't care for her husband or feed him, so he has to go and eat in the houses of other men. Where does she go all day long, to see other men or what? Now you've come to visit, what does she have that she can give you? Her genitals or her apron? If the man were here he could give you things, but she doesn't look after him, so he has gone away and won't be giving you anything, and there is no point in your visiting here."

5 / Special Foods

Before, when we made our gardens we did not have many good kinds of food. We had different sorts of the long *pit-pit* plant,[1] bananas,[2] sugarcane,[3] greens,[4] and short *pit-pit*.[5] Some of these varieties belonged to the forest areas and others to the grassland or valley places, some to the gardens where the trunks of giant beech trees[6] stood, and others to lower down where we planted the casuarina trees in fallow. The people who gardened up on the mountain and forest slopes used to bring down their particular varieties and exchange these for taro and cucumbers with the valley folk. Of our sweet potatoes, two kinds[7] belonged to the grasslands, and one to the hills.[8] We had two other old kinds also.[9]

Maize corn came to us only now, in my lifetime. Cabbages, tomatoes, onions, potatoes—all these are very recent. We did not have the Chinese taro,[10] the kind of dessert banana known as *rua mata,* or papaws. My father and grandfather ate none of these things.

We had no chickens, only pigs, just pigs. We had the dog too.

Those who lived in the Jimi Valley had numerous other kinds of taro, bananas, and the red and yellow pandanus fruits. If we had friends there we traveled down to get these from them.

I have said before what hard work we had with our tools of wood and stone, the men digging trenches with their spades of *yakla* (palm-wood) or casuarina wood, and the women coming behind to clear out the earth. If it was a forest garden, it was really tough going to clear the undergrowth and get it to burn, we had to slash again and again at branches and trunks until they were reduced to sections. That way it might take us the whole of one year to prepare the garden and it would be planted the next year. As we used our stone axes, the blades would fall out, or the binding would come off, and laboriously we had to put them together again. It was with much pain that we got our work done.

---

[1] *Ropin pep, ropin kupiti, ropin nggon.*

[2] *Rua mopa, rua rukmömb, rua keninga, rua membokl, rua mare.*

[3] *Po rarama, po pakla, po kaemb, po mowi, po mönggapa, po muklimb.*

[4] *Kim kundi, kim kimbi, kim ngönt, kim weka, kim kenggopa.*

[5] *Mui.*

[6] *Nde kraep.*

[7] *Oka rokle* and *oka opa; rokle* was planted when a garden was first made and *opa* used for the second planting.

[8] *Oka por,* which has a white tuber.

[9] *Oka kikamb* and *oka ketakae.*

[10] *Me tawe.*

Only the man who was strong was able to provide for his own food; the man who was not up to it would go crying for his food elsewhere and sleep hungry, hanging his head. In the forest the trees and tough creepers overhung the ground and outside of it the cane-grass stood up tall and stiff. We had no sharp tools to tackle them with. Sometimes we would have to go searching in old gardens for bits of *pit-pit*, seeds left behind, or inferior small sweet potatoes. Hunger, then, used to gnaw at our stomachs, and we thought of the possibility of getting lost in the bush and dying.

While I was growing up, the white man's things came to us and my father and others of his age said to me, "Oh, if only I was young now and could look forward to enjoying these things as you will do, but I am old and am going to die soon. We had so much pain and such hard times before, but now you're going to have all these things and die happy. If only these things could have reached us earlier!"

First we saw steel axes and bushknives, later we saw saucepans too. We said, "Oh, before we had to cut down trees and build fires, heat stones to make our ovens. If it was wet the food was spoiled, we would have to throw the greens away. The stones had to be heated properly, otherwise the oven wouldn't work. But now this saucepan is here all we have to do is fill it with water, build a small fire, and the water will boil to cook our food quickly." Now the younger people take all these things for granted and they don't realize how hard it was before, how difficult and worrying life was in the old days for their fathers and grandfathers.

The only distant place we could visit ourselves to get special products was the Jimi Valley. Once I went down there with two clansmen, Karakl and Mel. We went down to a place[11] where they were cooking some of those pandanus fruits I mentioned, and we wanted to get the grease of these fruits to decorate ourselves for courting parties. It was at the place of Mel's father, Ndekane,[12] and so Mel was cooking the fruits and extracting their oil. He took a big quantity of the oil and gave it to his mother and father, leaving me out, even though I and the others had helped him with the work of cooking. "All right," I thought. I saw how he had just put three full measures of oil into a bamboo tube and laid this aside. He asked me to get some water and pour it onto the fruit which we were mixing up for ourselves to eat.[13] I went over to that bamboo as if it contained water and tipped all of the oil out over the fruit. "Hey! Stop! You've poured out my oil!" he shouted. "Oh! Oh! I didn't know, I thought there was water in it!" I exclaimed. "Why didn't you look and see it was oil and save half of it, at least?" he asked. "I didn't watch what I was doing, I was looking at them sorting out the greens." Mel walked about, whistled, stared, and looked annoyed, while I covered my head with my hands and said how ashamed I was. While I did so I looked round for a stick or a stone with which to defend myself if he attacked me and thought, "It doesn't

---

[11] Called Kopakana.

[12] (In warfare some of the Kawelka used to flee as refugees to the Jimi. They planted groves of pandanus trees and maintained these subsequently by visits.)

[13] (The fruit has large numbers of seeds. These are kneaded in water to release the oily red or yellow pulp around them. The seeds are sucked and then spat out.)

matter if we fight because the other men will close in and stop us." The others kept silent and pretended not to have noticed.

At last Mel said, "That oil was being kept for you as a present for helping me, but now you've gone and tipped it all out. What will you do?" So I replied, "Oh, I thought I had got into trouble because it was someone else's, but if it was for me anyway, I've tipped out my own oil and it doesn't matter after all." I knew he was lying and he hadn't intended to give it to me. Afterwards the men told me they were all angry with him for not sharing out his oil and they were delighted with what I had done, as if it were something I had done on behalf of them all. They congratulated me and offered to pay me something for doing it.

6 / War

Now I want to talk about how we fought. Sometimes we fought with sticks. If a woman was raped she would scream out and come home covered in mud. Then her menfolk would go out together and seize pigs from the nearest house of the rapist's group or wait for them behind a turning and set on them with sticks. These were big long cudgels which each man cut for himself and put aside. When they used them they all ran forward together in a row, the sticks poised above their heads. It looked like the rafters of a house or the long supports to which we bind sugarcane stalks. Heads and arms could be broken. We of Mandembo clan in Kawelka tribe fought with the Membo clan in this way, we pushed each other to and fro back into each other's territory. We did the same with the neighboring Tipuka clans, chasing them as far as the banks of the Möka river in the valley, and then they raced back at us and chased us back up the hill to home.

There were no courts of justice then. Only the big-men could step in between the fighters, call to either side to keep its distance and arrange for pigs to be paid as compensation for wounds inflicted.[1] Each side had to pay out this compensation to its own supporters, and many pigs were spent in this way. The blows could even be fatal.

When we fought in earnest, with lethal weapons, we went to the help of our friends also. We burnt houses, slashed banana trees, tore the aprons off women and raped them, axed big pigs, broke down fences; we did everything. We carried on until the place was emptied of resources. Our opponents' allies would come and do this to our own area behind our backs too, but we would take no notice. We carried on with the main battle to see who would win. We said, "We're in trouble, that is why they are 'eating' at our place, let them do so," and we didn't retaliate at the time. Secretly we decided to wait and see if the plunderers got themselves into similar kinds of trouble later. We watched for our chance, and when they were involved in a fight elsewhere, we went to help their enemies, we cut their bananas, raped their women and burnt their houses, while they were kept busy fighting. We ate and ate at their place until they were ready to defecate in fear about it, but their opponents wouldn't let them turn back to drive us off. "Come here and fight. Where do you think you're going? You can't rush off like that," they said. In this way we paid back our injuries.

When we left our women behind and went out to fight, they were in danger. Men came to find them, chasing them down to the edges of streams till they seized hold of them, especially if their bodies were good to look at. Twenty men

---

[1] This kind of compensation we call *mongaemb*.

might lay hold of the same woman, pulling her around for a day and a night, and then letting her go, saying, "We've had intercourse with you, but you're not dead, so it doesn't matter, you can go home now."

To guard against this, our own allies used to give protection to our women and children, taking them to their own settlements and warning the enemies not to try an attack on them. Around their houses they put up special fences and taboo signs warning against intrusion, with a penalty of death. If the allies were strong like this, we were able to rejoin our women after the fighting was over. We returned to the charred remnants of our houses, cut timber and rebuilt them, mended fences, replanted the bananas, and our friends would give us back our women, children, netbags, grease-flasks, and pigs. Then we raised the pigs until they were fat and numerous, and when we were ready we said that now we must remember our allies, for if we didn't, next time they would side with our enemies and finish us off. So we cooked big pigs for them, making separate piles of pork for each small group, and in our speeches we said:

> You held the ropes of my pigs,
> You cared for my netbags and flasks,
> With the palms of your hands
> You protected my women's genitals
> While I was fighting.
> Now I am making this thing clean from myself.
> Take this pork and eat it,
> Now the debt between us is over.

When we fought we also built a special communal men's house.[2] After the fighting was over we dismantled the house but preserved its center post, which we laid down in a wet place. When we were ready to pay our allies for their help we said, "We are going to lift up the spirit trestle[3] now." Our visitors came and sat cross-legged in a row on our ceremonial ground, and we piled pork up in front of them—legs, heads, backbones—until the heaps rose to the level of their bird-of-paradise headdresses and then above those to the marsupial tails,[4] which they wore right on the top. Then we said, "See, our guests are no longer visible, we have hidden them with pork." We made to them the kind of speech I have just mentioned; let me tell you again:

> You placed your hands in protection
> Against our women's genitals.
> You cleaned out the cooking trench which had been fouled,
> You threw out the urine they placed in our drinking tubes,
> You helped me when they cut
> The bark belt off my body as I fought,
> With warm cordyline leaves
> You stroked our women's legs after they were raped.

---

[2] Called *el klaka manga*.
[3] *Kor paka.*
[4] *Kui weipö.*

Now our gifts of pork to you
Overtop the decorations on your head.
Let the enemies who fought us come and look at them.
This is all for you who showed your sympathy to us.
If the enemies don't do likewise for their friends,
Then I have beaten them.
If any of our enemies are here,
Let them go quickly.
"You enemies," we will say, "you took our girls,
You seized our pigs,
You stole our food.
What have you come to look at here? Go away!"
This pork is for those who helped us.

When someone died, it was often in fighting or by an enemy's sorcery, and we would think of revenge. At the funeral one of the men would pretend that the dead man's spirit had entered him; he shook and said, "Ha, ha, ha, ha!" When we saw this we thought that the spirit might help us to get revenge. We buried the body near to the surface of the ground, not too far down, for we thought that otherwise his spirit would not be able to emerge and help us in obtaining revenge. Eventually the body rotted, and we gathered the bones and head and placed them in a spirit house, and there we sacrificed pigs, calling to all the ghosts by name, all the men and women who had died. We told the male ghosts to eat the men's parts of the pig, the female ones the women's parts, so that we should not be sick and so that they would turn aside the enemy's spears aimed against us. We left none of the ghosts out, we spoke all their names, including those in our fathers' fathers' generation. We spoke the names of our senior-in-laws too if they were dead. We called on them all to come and be in front of us as a protection:

Let not the gardens we have planted fail,
Let not the pigs we have reared fall sick,
My taro that I have planted,
My yams that I have planted,
My bananas,
You people may come and eat and eat
And help us.
So that our pigs, our gardens, our people
Should not be sick and fail.
So that in fighting we shall not
Suffer spear wounds or arrow wounds,

Eat, eat, and eat
And come to our aid.

The sacrificer held the rope of his pig near to the grave of his dead father or elder brother, with the fire ready lit to singe the pig's carcass. As soon as he had finished speaking he told the men to club the pig. He himself would take the pig's head to a little "spirit men's house" as a special sacrifice for his father or brother or own children who might have died, and he would pray to them:

This is specially for you,
This is the pig's head I am giving you.
Let me not die by sorcery,
Let me not die by spear or arrow,
Let not a rotten tree fall and kill me,
Let me not die by fire inside a burning house.
You yourselves come and stand straight in front of me,
Come and be at my lips and at my eyebrows.
Eat this head
And help me.

Some time later perhaps our desire to kill an enemy would be gratified, and we said, "My word has come true, my ghost helped me and I have struck him." Then we put on fresh cordyline leaves, rubbed our skin with pig-grease, and danced in delight and sang:

I've killed him,
Now I'll cook him.
Lay him out
And eat him.[5]

They looked over to the place where people were mourning their dead man and waved, saying, "What's the matter, why are you crying? I'm pleased with some food I've eaten over here!" We made them furious by saying things like this. Later on, of course, it might be the other way around, and they would rejoice, go courting girls, and sing loudly in our faces. It was a matter of sheer rivalry between ourselves and others; we bickered and dickered incessantly like dogs shut in a pen.

In those days all the Tipuka clans were at war with all the Kombukla. The Kawelka joined with the Tipuka as their allies, and all the Minembi clans joined with the Kombukla as their allies.[6] On one occasion, as I heard, our men went out to fight the Kombukla at a swampy place called Kitip near their boundary with the Tipuka. It was difficult, boggy ground with dense stands of cane-grass, and only a few of our men made their way through to help. The enemy routed our side and killed several of our men,[7] chased them back as far as Mbukl and then turned for home.

Among our own Kawelka men, Kur and Ik, whom I mentioned at the beginning of my account,[8] were both fine young men who were killed. Their mother, who was of Tipuka Kendike clan, was deeply upset. Ik, in particular, had been a handsome man. He used to play the bamboo flute, and people came from all

---

[5] This was only in the song. We didn't actually eat the man.

[6] (The full picture was rather more complicated than this "ground-plan," or summary, suggests. See A.J. Strathern, *The Rope of Moka,* 1971, chap. 3. Cambridge University Press.)

[7] (Ongka cited 20 men from 10 different clans in the Tipuka-Kawelka alliance. These, he said, were the most important men of those killed; how could he remember those who were less important?)

[8] (See the beginning of chapter 1.)

around to listen to it, telling others to stop chattering so they could attend with care. At her place, Kenan Manga, the mother sang a lament for Ik:

Ik, oh my Ik,
Ik, my Ik,
Ik, oh my Ik,
Ik, of the place Kenan,[9] is killed.
His flute is broken now.

"Who was it killed him?" they asked, and the answer was "Kombukla Ndoa with his cassowary-claw-tipped spear." So two brothers of our clan, Ndekane and Roklpa, went up to one of our settlement places which is high up in the forest, to the place Okla, and fixed up a cassowary trap at the foot of a giant wild pandanus tree, where its tough fruits fell down. They placed some excrement there and nearby a noose. A cassowary came and smelt at the place and its neck was trapped in the noose. They removed its claws to make the points for their own spears. However, they did not go themselves, but sent two other men first with the new spears, Öi and Nikint. These two were to attack the Kombukla by stealth at night. They set off up to the place Konde,[10] and at dawn they stationed themselves silently by the doorway of Ndoa's men's house. But Ndoa, as big-men used to do in those days, had gone to sleep in a secret house. Leaving less important men to guard the main men's house, the big-men made hideouts in low-lying spots screened from sight and near to the women's lavatory places. At night they quietly stole out, waving a burning stick as if they were women going to the lavatory. Then in the very early morning they crept back again and were seen talking in the men's house as if they had slept the night there. So that morning it was not Ndoa who came out of the men's house in the early morning, but an unimportant man.[11] As he did so, the cassowary claw pierced his neck and he fell back into the hearth with a cry.

The two attackers ran off in opposite directions. Nikint met Ndoa, who had heard the cry and emerged from his hiding place, and pierced him in the chest. He ran on but he was surrounded. In the half-light the Kombukla asked him what he was up to. "I'm a Minembi man running away because the Kawelka are coming to attack us," he said, but they lit a torch and recognized him. In their anger they cut him to pieces and placed the remains on a fire like the trestles of wood we use to heat stones for cooking pork, and his bones were burnt to cinders.

Öi escaped. Nikint's relatives were angry with him and attacked him for taking Nikint off and getting him killed. They broke his head open with stick blows. They took hold of his wife and raped her repeatedly, keeping her outside in the bush for days. Finally they burnt his house down. They also beat Ndekane and Roklpa for sending the two men off. That episode was finished.

Then warfare broke out between those of the Minembi who live down below us to the west, the Andakelkam, and ourselves. The Minembi came up by the pathway

---

[9] (The place name itself means "song.")

[10] (This is now part of Kawelka Kundmbo clan territory. Previously, one of the Kombukla clans lived there. Its men were eventually driven out by the Kundmbo.)

[11] Called Ndiproembömbil, "Fire-stick-holder."

near to one of our cemeteries, Koklnge. They came right up into our settlement places; men who watched said they came as far as the place Epamekui. So they fought up and down, backwards and forwards. Four men on the Minembi side were killed, one of Kombukla and the other a Klamakae ally, the other two were Minembi. After this the Minembi and the Klamakae went to the Tipuka over to our east and bribed them, offering them wives for nothing and payments of wealth if they would assassinate one of the Kawelka for them in revenge for these deaths. The Oklembo clansmen took them up on this and came out against us with spears and shields, saying as a pretext that we had killed one of their men by sorcery. We denied it, saying, "We were allies of yours in the big fighting against the Minembi, your comrades in arms. Why should we kill one of your men?" But their minds were full of the new reward the Minembi had promised them and they said, "No, you killed him." "All right," we said, and joined battle. All of the Kawelka rallied at the cemetery place known as Kenankormanga and there, as the Oklembo advanced on us, one of our men shot an Oklembo man, Kundi Kongrui, straight in the eye and killed him. Then the Oklembo called on the other Tipuka clans to help them and they surrounded us completely. It was very dry weather and they set light to the scrub to burn us out. We kept smothering the fires while they lit more.

By night they advanced again and drove us out. Flames from the fires raced up the hills and we ran for it, up the Ombil stream, up the Möka river to the mountains. Our women and children scattered too, then, and ran wherever they could, while we headed for the forest like wild pigs. The Klamakae tribesmen, who were helping the Minembi, came up from the west around the northern end of our land, and there they found two of our men, Oni and Kalimb, lying wounded at the place Kiningangmul. The Oklembo too ran along the edge of the rivers and at Pilpana they found one of our big-men, Klönt, who had been wounded in the back by a falling tree and was lying in his house, and they killed him. The Tipuka as a whole laid waste to our territory, cut bananas, burnt houses, slaughtered pigs, seized our wives and ripped the aprons off them, carried them naked around the place, and had intercourse with them at will, sleeping in nests out in the open.

One woman carried her little daughter deep into the forest. It was very hot and there was no water. At night the two slept outside and the mother felt thirsty again as she gave the child the breast. She tried to squeeze some water from moss but none came. In the end she took a leaf and folded it to catch the daughter's urine, and she drank this as it flowed. Her parched mouth was softened and she slept. Next morning she looked down and saw all the houses razed to the ground in her husband's place, so the two of them stayed up there, in their hunger eating shoots from the *neng* tree and leaves of the *mit* plant, like marsupials.

Next day our allies from the Jimi, Tipuka Ndikambo clansmen and men of Palke tribe, sent out search parties for our women and children, bringing them all together from their separate hiding places to see how many had died. The survivors they took away to the place Kopakana, where there are great boulders beside a stream, and there they looked after them. So it is that nowadays they say in speeches to us:

When your enemies saw smoke from your fires,
We told them it was only a cloud.
When they saw your footsteps in the forest,
We said that dogs had been passing by that way.
We placed our hands as a protection
Over your women's genitals.
You should think of us, but now
You are not doing so.

That is what they say to us when they want us to give them things in recognition of their help before.

We, the men, returned to the communal men's house in Kenankormanga. We had to stay and fight it out. Our cross-cousins from other groups brought in our dead for us and buried them. We had to stay put. Where could we go? Back into our mothers' vaginas? Or could we run away like boys and join another group? No, we said, we would stay. If they killed our pigs, well, we had eaten pigs before; if they had intercourse with our women, well, we had had intercourse with them before too; if they burnt our houses, we could rebuild them. Let them try to kill us one by one until we were all finished off and a visitor to our land could later tell the story of how the Kawelka all stood together as one man and were annihilated at this spot. The older men stood up and made powerful talk: "Let us stand here and face them, let us take the wounds in our fronts and not in our backs fleeing, let our women escape with their small sons at the breast, and later bring them back to show them the place where we, the men of Kawelka, fought and died to the last man, so they will know who their fathers were and who it was that killed them." This was the kind of talk the older men made to strengthen the resolve of us younger men, otherwise we would truly be routed and destroyed.[12]

We were surrounded completely by the Oklembo; their shields, their bunches of spears, their white cockatoo feather headdresses were everywhere. There was nothing to eat. We pulled taro shoots but these were soon finished. We dug the planted stocks of sugarcane and these were finished. We ate *kenggopa* greens and these were finished. We were forced to eat mushrooms, tree fungi, fern leaves. There was no sweet potato; all the gardens were burned off. In the days of warfare we did not have big gardens at the best of times, and now we had none. Hunger tore at our insides and our eyes closed in pain. Older men pushed leaves into their bark belts to fill out the space between their stomachs and their belts. They declared they were pleased to be hungry and went out to fight again.

We retired to a place higher up, above Kiningangmul, where it was dry and stony, and the enemies cut off all access to gardens below us. We finished all the greens, shoots, mushrooms, vines, and leaves; there was nothing more to eat, and we sat with heads down, able to forget our hunger only at night when we slept exhausted. All this time we had to keep fighting. The enemy came with drawn bow,

---

[12] These older men were Kindi, Mara, Kilwa, Kaepa, Ndekane, Roklpa, Akel, Koi, Eya, Nui, Ndat, Öndipi, Pana, Tei, Manga, Ok, Waima, Kakl, Kindwa, Pena, Reipa, Kiti, and Korlop; these were the men who told us boys we had to stick it out.

we faced him and drove him back, then he drew his bow and came forward again. Eyes were put out and legs were lamed; we had to cut out arrows stuck fast in flesh. Something like a month passed by, then two, three, four, and in the fifth month both sides were tired of it and began to slacken. Then the Kawelka were able to scatter and go off into the forests, hunting for marsupials and shooting birds. The Oklembo men too rested.

One day some of the Oklembo who lived down in the Jimi Valley to the north came to visit the others and these went to meet them. Some Kawelka were hunting in the forest at the same time and both sides suddenly came face to face. Both thought they had been ambushed and quickly opened fire. There were woundings all around and the Oklembo ran off to the Jimi with their clansmen. Ukl, who was only a boy then, came racing down, covered in the yellow clay we use for mourning at funerals, and told us they had been ambushed. We sprinted down to the warhouse to get our shields and spears, saying, "Let's see if any of them are at home!" We charged over to their settlements. In surprise they shouted, "Hey, the Kawelka are coming to attack us!" It was too late. We swept over them, raped their women standing up, chopped bananas, axed pigs, fired houses. They fled like wild pigs from all their settlements.

That night a Tipuka man of Eltimbo clan was searching for a pig to kill as plunder from behind the Oklembo ranks, and he came upon a pig's nest. He poked at it and thought he felt a pig, but in fact it was a woman, who had taken refuge there in fear when the fighting broke. "Who's that?" she said. She rushed out and clasped him and said, "Don't kill me!" Then, "Oh, it's you" (recognizing him). "Come and sleep with me in here. Never mind about pigs."[13]

These events are remembered in our ceremonial speeches. The Oklembo say to us, "We drove you out and your mothers had to drink their daughters' urine." We reply, "We drove you out and your old women had to clasp men and sleep with them in pigs' nests." It was true that in those days all a woman could do to save herself in war was to offer her vagina to a man, that was the only strong thing she had to act like a shield in front of herself and avoid being killed.

While the other Kawelka men brought up the rear, Ukl ran through the hot hillsides like a cassowary chick over to Mbukl and told the rest of the men who were gathered there, setting traps and watching for birds. He shouted that the Oklembo had set an ambush, so they rushed for their weapons and drove the Tipuka out of their settlements, with an impact like a bamboo tube exploding and flying in different directions.[14] Up to the tops of the hills the Tipuka fled, while the Kawelka made havoc below. After they had satisfied themselves with destroying property and assaulting the women sexually, the Kawelka men said, "All right, you chased us to the hills and our women had to drink their daughters' urine. Now you'll have to stroke the genitals of your women with warm leaves to soothe them after we have torn them apart in intercourse. Now there is no quarrel between us, let us separate and be quiet."

---

[13] (Names omitted.)
[14] (Bamboo tubes do this if heated.)

So the Kawelka gradually returned from their forest shelters, rebuilt their settlements, and raised pigs. The Oklembo did the same. Four years or thereabouts
passed by, then each side separately held pig killings to make returns to their allies, who had brought them food or had protected their women. To all these men
they gave legs and backbones of pork, saying to each what he had done for them.
"You showed our people your fallow gardens, your new gardens, you saved them
and this is to thank you," they said, and piled the heaps higher with stomachs, livers, backbones. We gave separately also to the cousins who had helped us in the
actual fighting. When we were threatened they had run forward and chased the
assailant away, seized him, barred his way, speared him, and averted the danger.
So these too we invited to come and thanked them for saving our lives. We were
especially grateful to those who had looked after our wives and children and we
gave plenty to them. We used big shields in warfare, made from the *reipö* tree and
called by its name. Men cut down the big tree and removed a section from it,
shaping it at top and bottom. Then they fastened pincers as a vise on it and lashed
these tight with vines and heated the wood over a fire. As the sap oozed out they
struck it with the butt of the axes and poured water over it to make the sap come
out completely and leave the wood hard. They stood on it to keep it straight and
heated it several times till it was quite tough. Then they painted it and attached
holders to it at the edge and at the middle.[15]

The heavy shield was this *reipö* and there was another lighter one called
romakl. The man who carried *romakl* would collect arrows to use, a large selec-
tion of different kinds. While the men with heavy shields went forward into combat against the enemy's spears, the *romakl* man scouted at their backs or along the
edges of their advance, looking to see if an enemy should expose a hand, leg, face,
or body part and thus supply a target. The *reipö* men locked their shields tightly
together in a long row in order to baffle and dazzle[16] their opponents, hoping to
leave no gap through which arrows could penetrate. If anyone did expose a knee,
an eye, the crown of his head, an arrow would be put through it at once.

Then his friends would have to remove him. They carried him away hurriedly and held him down while they cut into his flesh with bamboo knives to
reach the barbed arrow head and pull it out. If it was in only a short way they
seized it with their teeth and extracted it. If it was in deeper they used two dried
claws of the eagle bird to help them. Its claws are very tough and they dried
them out by keeping them in the house. With these they held back the cut-away
flesh while they searched down for the exact place where the arrow point was
embedded. "Stop it, I'm dying in pain," the man would say, but they kept on
searching. Or they took a tough old pig bone and split slivers off it. These they
used as pincers to grasp the arrow, then bound them tightly together with a vine
and so pulled the head out.

---

[15] Arrowheads we made from strong *yakla* wood, also obtained in the forest. These had to be
cut straight and fixed into cane shafts with some tacky material packed round to keep the heads
tightly in place.

[16] This was called *ndinja*, a term we use also for a waterfall and for the cassowary plumes we
fixed at the top of shields.

Wounds were left open in this way, and we had no medicine in those days. However, we used to pack a wound with *nggökön* leaves and put a banana sheath over it. It would rot and fester and pus would come out, but after that it might heal up. If not, we would watch the wound until it rotted badly and the bone inside was infected and became dark in color. The pus went back into the man's flesh, and then we said he would die.

7 / Attracting Wealth

I will talk about fighting and death again later. We had some peaceful customs too.

One thing we did was for very young children, whose skin was soft and tender. Their mothers used to line the netbags in which they carried them around with the soft round leaves of the *koki*[1] plant as a bed for them in the first days of their life. As soon as the baby's navel string was cut, the baby was laid in leaves arranged on an old pandanus mat. When it was a little bigger, it was placed in a small new mat and a better-made netbag. Now its mother would search for fine dry leaves from special trees.[2] They dried these carefully, then broke them up to make a soft bed, which was brightly colored too. They placed these leaves into a netbag lined with marsupial fur, used for carrying the child around by day. (A different netbag was used at night.) They fashioned sets of pig tusks and in between these they put bright red seeds[3] and on top of these a moth cocoon. This arrangement would be placed at the bottom of the netbag and the dried leaves placed on top. As the mother went by people said, "How bright! The spirit is all there! That child will not get sick. She has borne a fine child and carries it in her netbag with pigs' tusks arranged in a navel design and red seeds." However, if the design was incomplete or lopsided, people would criticize it.

We did some kind things for old people too. When parents grew old, a son or a married daughter would say, "Our parent is going to die. Let us cook a pig and pay him our respects."[4] So they harvested taro and yam tubers and took a big pig and cooked it. When they opened up the oven, they took out a front leg, fat from the belly, and the top part of the backbone and gave it to the parent, saying, "When I was small you cleaned my excrement and urine, you stopped me from falling in the fire, you sheltered me from the hot sun, you obtained a wife for me when I was big. Now you are old and sit beside the fire. Eat this pork and do not feel angry with me; eat it and feel good. Later, when you are dead, do not visit me with sickness, don't be upset, don't make my children ill. Feel good about this; this is my last present to you. I am giving it to you while you are still alive, so eat it and be happy and die contented and don't make us sick after your death." If there was an old man who had no sons and lived by himself, his group-mates would similarly go to him and say, "If you die and leave your things behind, other

---

[1] (Also used for chewing with betel nut nowadays.)
[2] *Pokil, pokoklma, lkaemba, pon,* and *niki.*
[3] *Kela kur.*
[4] *Rawe ngamon.*

people will come and take them and you will be made upset by this." So they would cook his own pig for him, and he ate it and shared it as he wished to do, and later he died. We did the same for old women too.

Most of the time we were anxious to secure and build up wealth for exchanges. Ritual experts came and made spells for us around the center post of our men's house. The expert took a cassowary-bone dagger he had and said, "Some men have planted stakes in your ground. Now I'll make a spell and dig them out for you." He meant that rival ritual experts had secretly planted little stakes in our ground to prevent wealth from coming to us; it would be deflected and go elsewhere. These he would now remove. He came with a kit of *kuklumb* leaves, eagles' claws, and cassowary bones in his small netbag. One expert among us Kawelka was Membo Pokl, among the Tipuka there was Ndakla of Kendike clan, and there was Papeke Ndekanga from Minembi. When one of these men was to perform, people came from long distances with food, even in from the Jimi Valley, with bananas, taro, yams, small pigs, and fish caught in traps. The owners of the men's house where the performance was to take place walked around asking for shells which they could display at the far end of the house and later get pigs in exchange for them. This was especially done at new ceremonial grounds, which we used to lay out like small airfields.

Here a man might build a new ceremonial men's house surrounded by cordylines and a special set of shrubs planted in a tub right in front of its central door.[5] We decorated this tub with pig-grease and charcoal; in its middle we planted a cordyline, and we used soot and yellow earth to decorate this. We added the bones of pigs we had cooked in sacrifices and bunches of *kuklumb* leaves until the whole thing was an impressive sight. We told people not to go near it for we were making spells over it.

Meanwhile the future recipients of the moka gifts which we planned to make would give us heads and legs of pork and bunches of bananas as anticipatory presents. The intended chain of persons and groups to be involved was a very long one, and the men at the end of the line would send gifts down it and these would change hands until our own nearest partners brought them as gifts for us. The man who was going to make moka decorated the center post of the new house with *kuklumb* leaves and set out the shells he had collected in rows right down to the entrance way, row above row, dusted with red ocher and surrounded with those same *kuklumb* leaves. The partners brought in their presents and said, "Here you are, now it's up to you to make moka to us. I will soon be an old man; now is the time for you to make returns to us."

"All right," he would say. "Now let us finish the work on the men's house, and tomorrow you can hear what I have to say and go home." He lined up the pigs for killing and felled them. Bananas were peeled, greens gathered, and the ovens prepared. The cooked food was then divided into portions and laid in the men's house, and the men were told to guard it without stealing from it. Then they put the strong *towakl* creeper around the center post and the ritual expert sang:

---

[5] *Malt* and *koepa* trees were planted in this tub, which we called the *pokla mbo*. It was bound with tough *towakl* vines and the earth smoothed away on either side of the doorway.

I lash the vine,
I lash the vine,
I lash the *tui* vine.
I lash the vine,
I lash the vine,
I lash the *towakl* vine.
I lash the vine,
I lash the vine,
At the end of the pearl shell.
I lash the vine,
I lash the vine,
With the big tusker.
I lash the vine,
I lash the vine . . .

And so on. He went round and round the central post lashing it with the *towakl* creeper until it was daybreak and the first birds were calling. Then the men shook bunches of *kuklumb* leaves inside the house, brushing and singing:

Oh the kuklumb leaves
I fasten,
I fasten them to the navel.
I brush with them
To the end of the pearl shell.
I fasten the kuklumb.
Oh, the kuklumb leaves!
I fasten
In the small men's house.
I fasten,
I brush,
In the small men's house.
I fasten
The handle of the pearl shell.
I fasten
The rope of the cowrie shells.
I fasten,
I brush . . .

Then they stopped and prepared to divide out the pork.

The next day they decorated and the moka-maker displayed his shells, show-ing them to separate partners in sets of eight or ten, and for each set he was enti-tled to add a bamboo stick to the tally he wore in front of his chest, the *koa mak,* so that it went down and down until it was very long. In some cases it would reach to the ground, then the people would say he was truly a big-man, unlike those whose tallies were shorter. When they were to dance, his friends would bring decorations, all kinds of feathers and shells, face paint, bailer shells and plumes, enough for the women too. The men had to prepare their wide horned wigs also. When all was ready at last, the moka-maker killed more pigs and distributed to those who had brought decorations. He brought out his own big pigs and shells and placed one large shell upright at the ceremonial tub; then the others were laid down in a long row, with marks to indicate which partners they were intended for. "Let me see how long the line will be," he said. Then another man put down his shells to continue the line, it went down and down until it came right to the tail end of the ceremonial ground.

The man making his moka went to the side of the ground and removed his tall plumes to put on cassowary-feather topknots instead. He placed numbers of these on his head,[6] took special leaves[7] for his rear covering, and decorated himself all over with black charcoal. A watching man gave the signal: "He's ready now!" He rushed out and they called to the crowd to give way. In one hand he held an adz decorated with leaves and in the other he held ferns. Anyone who got in his way was trampled down. With a swishing sound he raced to the bottom of the ceremonial ground, then back up to its head, where he made his speech: "I made this ceremonial ground a long time ago. The cordyline bushes that line it are grown tall, the trees in the ceremonial tub are tall. Now I am releasing my gifts to you. From whatever direction you come—south, east, north, west—you may take your gifts off now. You have brought me solicitory presents of pigs and shells, you have waited and suffered much pain. Now I am holding the rope and giving it to you. Take it off, make more moka, eat it, pay a bride-wealth, do whatever you like with it. Now my task is over, I'm removing my decorations, I shall be going off into the bush and doing my own garden work."

So saying, he took off his decorations and hung them on the tree in the tub. So he gave his moka and the recipients took it off and made theirs, and their recipients made theirs, and so it was carried out, out, out, and out to far distant places, while the first moka-maker returned to his garden work, to pig breeding, to gathering a few shells from bride-wealths for his daughters, saving up the wealth until at last he had enough to put on a show again. He reworked the fallow gardens, grew bananas, sugarcane, and sweet potatoes, and his pigs were fat. He gathered shells from partners this way and that, to and fro, until he had sufficient amounts for a moka and was able to add more slats to his tally, one slat for each set of eight or ten shells until it went down further and further and became immensely long. So he stayed at his place, built his ceremonial men's houses, decorated himself, decorated his women, and performed his rituals.

I did those kinds of things too. I gave moka to everyone, to the Tipuka, Minembi, Kombukla, my own Kawelka—so many times! Everyone said, "Let's go and see Ongka-Kaepa," if they wanted to raise some wealth for an occasion. My own long tally is hanging on the wall of my house now; it's as long as the wall itself, but I'm embarrassed to wear it now that the white men are here. I had partners in distant places, from the Jimi, from the eastern valleys where the Kendipi tribesmen live, from the uplands near Hagen; they brought big pigs down to me and slept out in the open before returning. The Hagen men brought me cassowary headdresses and packs of salt, of the round or long kind.[8] The Jimi people brought plumes of the white bird of paradise, eagle feathers, parrot feathers, woven decorations for bark

---

[6] (These were a sign of his making shell moka.)
[7] *Kuklnga.*
[8] (Traded in from the Enga area to the west.)

belts, cassowaries, packs of sago. The eastern valley men brought plumes of the red bird of paradise, white marsupial furs, parrot wings. Even Enga men came to see me, with big marsupials and necklaces of cowrie shells. They brought all these things and I acted as a middleman, switching things round between them, giving things from the Jimi people to the Hagen men and vice versa, and so on, so that people said, "He is in the middle of us all and he is generous." From all sides they came to me, and I also used what they brought for my own moka-making and bride-wealth payments.

My last wife, Mande, married me very recently, some years after Andrew had come to my place.[9] When he came, he asked me to tell him the meaning of everything, so I set off telling him about how we fight, cook pigs, get wives, make moka, make speeches, use straightforward or concealed forms of talk, get ourselves into trouble, get ourselves out of trouble, tell others off, speak straight to them, speak indirectly to them; how some people are tough and others soft, how people kill others secretly by sorcery or openly by violence, and how people behave when they are sorry for others. Andrew listened to it all and said, "Yes, I understand." After a while he said, "You do really strong things, but there's just one thing you do which is a rubbishy thing, that is killing people by sorcery, you should stop doing that. All the things you do with people who are alive around you are good, but you shouldn't think of killing people."[10] He spoke to me as one who gives advice and I listened to him.

I carried on making my moka ceremonies. Men came to praise me for these and I paid them for their praise, as is customary with us. I gave fifty kina[11] to the old big-man, Kitepi Kuri, father of Parua, the MP, I gave a white bird-of-paradise plume and three pounds in money to Kumndi Mel, another old big-man. I gave three pounds to Kitepi Wai (a young big-man). Kendike Mit praised me and I gave him fifty kina.[12] These men said to me, "There are no ponds and swamps in your place for pigs to forage in. It is a place of cane-grass stands where clouds hang heavy and tree-stumps are rooted stubbornly in the hard ground. How do you manage to raise so many pigs?" Most recently (1974) when I brought out my big pigs to give to the Member of Parliament Parua, he just accepted them quietly without asking for any more as exchange partners usually do.[13] The first pig I placed at the head of the row was the one which I called Rut Pepa, the next was Poklök Wane, the next Rut Wane, the next Waimorong Pokl.[14] Then there were

[9] (Andrew Strathern came in early 1964. The last wife married Ongka in 1974. She was a widow of long standing who decided she liked Ongka and wanted to stay with him. Despite some protests from her sons, Ongka kept her.)

[10] (Andrew Strathern does not recall specifically saying this to Ongka, but perhaps he did, as a part of the numerous conversations over a period of years.)

[11] (The kina is Papua New Guinea's unit of currency, established in 1975 at par with the Australian dollar. At the time of which Ongka speaks here, people were actually using Australian pounds as currency.)

[12] (Mit is a cousin of men of Ongka's small group and thus in classificatory terms a cousin to him also.)

[13] (This gift was the subject of the film *Ongka's big Moka*.)

[14] (Big pigs are often named. The first three names are the places where the pigs were reared, the last a personal name.)

four big pigs without names. There were two valuable cassowary birds. There was a long tube of decorating oil. I myself paid for and gave away two cows.[15] The gifts of pigs I made were to Parua eight, Wai eight, Nukint eight, Kot eight, Raem eight, Pera eight, Mel eight, Ken and Pulti eight, Kuma two, and Mitipa two.[16]

This was the last strong thing of our own customs that I did. I have done these things with pigs, shells, cassowaries, and cattle. My moka tally hangs there getting dusty on the wall now. But I don't understand the things that the white men can do. They can speed through the water and the air. How do they do it and why?

[15] (Each cow cost at least $200 in Australian cash. They were presented in return for a number of cows received from the Tipuka clans in February 1965. The prestige of a moka occasion is greatly enhanced by the addition of extra gifts of this kind.)

[16] (Parua is a sister's son of the Kawelka and a pivotal exchange partner; Wai is a neighbor and a young big-man; Nukint is a neighbor and minor big-man of Kitepi clan; Kot was an in-law, neighbor and big-man of Eltimbo clan; Raem is Ongka's favorite and eldest daughter; Pera is a wife's sister's husband; Mel is the husband of a favorite sister Kokl; Ken is son of Ongka's sister Rambe; Pulti is a brother of the latest wife, Mande; Kuma is a councilor and big-man of Oklembo clan; Mitipa is the husband of Wora, sister of Ongka's dead favorite wife, Pau [see chap. 5].)

8 / The Firethong Test

We had methods of finding out about sorcery and of taking revenge for killings.

A man would go out to visit relatives or friends from another tribe and when he came back he might fall sick. They would call in ritual experts, but these could not cure him, so he died. "All right," they said, and buried his body on a trestle of leaves in the cemetery. They fenced the place around tightly, covered the corpse with leaves and branches, and went off, leaving just one man to guard the place. He waited for five days or so and then went to examine the corpse; if it was still lying out stiff and fresh, he covered it and returned home. On a visit like this he was afraid that the corpse's smell would get into his beard and hair, so he smoothed his hair with mud and shaved off his beard. This was so that at night he would not have to vomit from his own stench. After another five days he went again, and, finding the corpse had decayed, he pushed apart the flesh under the rib cage and searched for the stomach.

He scraped and cut away the rotten parts with a bamboo knife until he found the stomach. This he examined for parts which were dark and solid, and these he extracted and placed in banana and *mara* leaves. Then he covered the corpse again. These visits he always made at dawn.

His brothers asked him "Have you found anything yet?" He said, "Just a little something. Let's look at it carefully by ourselves." They went off secretly and spread out breadfruit leaves, then opened out the bundle, poured water on it, separated the pieces, turned them over, washed out the rotten fluids, and then they would see some greens, sweet potato, or taro fragments. Before the man died, they had asked him for details of all the food he ate on his visit away from the clan and who had given the food to him; and now they recognized the pieces of food he had spoken of. The dark bits were the poison or sorcery stuff that had been slipped in with the food to kill him.

They said nothing about this but wrapped the sorcery stuff carefully and hid it in a bamboo tube which they lodged under the eaves of a secluded spirit house used for sacrifices. The public funeral ceremonies they had conducted as if the man had simply died of sickness. Secretly they took the dead man's jaw and some other bones, and for these they built a special spirit men's house, constructing it firmly and in trim style with plenty of thatch, and at the top of its center post they placed the bones on a small platform supported on a nest of *mara* leaves, ferns, and moss. Underneath this they decorated the post with leaves as for an ordinary ceremonial men's house, and the outside was festooned with *mara* and *kundumb* leaves too. They cut a diamond-shaped hole in the doorway to let the man's soul go out and in. They called the house a "hornet," from its narrow top and wide bottom. The man who had found the "poison" now looked after this house. They made a sacrifice and gave him the pig's head to eat (or a whole side if the pig was a small one). They told the ghost that they were now going to visit friends and accept food from others, but the guardian would stay with him and not share food with anyone else.

To begin with, the guardian had eaten only hard bananas cooked in ashes and scraped, so as to stop himself from vomiting when he handled the corpse. Now he could eat pork, but only if he cooked it by himself on his own cooking stones. If he ate taro or marsupials, he cooked these on separate stones, which he then threw away.[1] He could butcher and cook pigs on behalf of the others but was not to swallow his saliva with the smell of pork on it, and had to wash his hands carefully afterwards. The others sent offers of rewards in pork and shells around secretly, in an effort to discover who the killer had been. When they discovered his name, they tried to lure him out by offers of presents, but he would guess their intentions and send only his womenfolk and other relatives to see them. The guardian grew tired of living by himself and not having a share in all the good foods the others ate, so his brothers made efforts to entice their suspect again: "I wonder if you'd like to come up to our place for a little ceremony?" The suspect answered directly: "I didn't kill your man. Why are you asking me this?" "Oh, we're embarrassed, it's just a little thing like a bird's song or the feces of a spirit, don't worry, it's nothing big. We're eating food together with you, and one of our children has fallen sick,[2] so come up and we'll try the firethong divination."

The suspect's people argued about whether to go or not, but eventually they went, preparing themselves for violence. The hosts brought out a hardened firethong and a tinder of *kuklumb* leaves,[3] and invited them to try it. At first they declined. At length, a big-man would come forward and say, "If there is trouble, we should not fight or kill in revenge. We have pigs and shells with which to pay compensation. Just try out the firethong." He made the talk cool in this way, and one man came forward to use the thong. If he successfully made fire, he went free, for he was accounted innocent. Perhaps he had cooked a pig as a sacrifice for his own ghosts and obtained their support! But if fire would not come or the thong broke, they would exclaim and set upon him at once.

It might not be possible to persuade the suspected man to come out and take the test. Then they would redouble their efforts to lure him out with promises of pigs and shells. They told his women and children how well disposed toward him they were. They would suggest to him, "Just come to a nearby hill with a stream in between us and we'll send people down with the gift for you." Meanwhile, they

---

[1] (All these precautions emphasized the guardian's separation from the others and his dedication to the ghost whose death was to be avenged. The others might be sharing food with relatives of the suspected killer, but the ghost and the guardian were not to be contaminated by such contact, so they were kept apart.)

[2] (This would be interpreted as a sign that the ghosts of relatives disapproved of them sharing food with the murderer of a kinsman.)

[3] (Such thongs were used to make fire by friction, by being rapidly sawed up and down against a piece of wood until a spark flew out and caught the tinder placed below. Here the firethong is used for a divination ritual.)

told other men to surround the area, hiding in grasses and undergrowth, and these positioned themselves accordingly, but the suspect would guess and call out from a more distant point that he was not coming.

The close relative of the dead man persisted. This time he filled a netbag with greens and placed in it the stalk of a banana bunch which looked just like a pig's trotter. He carried it over to a place near to the suspect's settlement, staggering as if it were heavy, and called out, "See this leg of pork I've brought you, I've just come by myself with it secretly, come down and get it." He had deployed a large number of men and they fanned out deep and wide around the spot. If the man was attracted down, the relatives seized him and the others quickly closed in and chopped him to pieces.

Whichever way they got their victim, the next day they prepared a ceremony in which they brought out the sorcery stuff which they had kept so carefully and so long. They displayed it on a special trestle bound round with the tough *towakl* creeper for the public to see, and they revealed the story of how they had tracked down their victim as the sorcerer. They told how they had questioned their own man before he died, identified the contents of his stomach, and afterwards learned the reports about who had rejoiced and decorated themselves after his death. "Now," they said, "we will come out of mourning. We will take the cassowary plumes, ax, and other relics of our man and wear these at dances."

They made a challenge to their victim's side to come and fight them if they wished. The new victim's relatives would say, if they wished to take up this challenge, "Why? The other death was a long time ago. He's killed my man for no good reason!" And they would bring out their spears and shields. But if they were tired of fighting they would let the matter be at first.

When this revenge had been successfully accomplished, the guardian of the secret spirit house would decorate himself with fine plumes and remove the skull and jaw of the dead man and place these carefully in the crook of a tree. Then he set fire to the spirit house. Now the new victim's kin would not forget the matter. They took a broken spear or ax of his and told his son to keep it hidden in his house. If the son built a new house, he was to transfer this relic to it; he was to keep it even if it was old and dirty, to pass it on to his own son as a sign that revenge must be taken if he did not complete the revenge himself. At a bride-wealth occasion, or a funeral, they were to go out and see a relative of the other side who was just like their own man who had been killed, in appearance and size, and they were to strike him down. When they had done this they too could take out the relic they had kept, display it, and finally burn it.

The warnings would now be going in the opposite direction. Much time could have passed, but no matter. The man who took his revenge first was warned, "You'll be killed. Be careful, don't walk around, stay at home." He heeded their advice, but after a long time he might grow tired of taking precautions and would try to find a way of making peace. He sent a message to the others: "Your man died a long time ago but you are still upset. I want to give you something." He offered pearl shells, ropes of cowries, decorating oil and pigs, and the others might decide to accept these as compensation. Then they would sacrifice to their dead man, saying, "My father gave your relics to me saying I was to avenge your death, but now this man has himself come forward to make peace and is giving us wealth, so I will throw out your relics and burn them now. There is no way after this by which I could kill him. I am going to make friends with him. Take our sacrifice now and do not be angry."

However, if the man refused to offer compensation they would watch out and surely kill him. Then they would rush home and prepare the celebration known as "eating the victim's liver." They entered their spirit house and took out the relics and announced the successful revenge-taking to the ghost. They butchered pigs, removed their livers and placed these on a trestle made of the *wilaula* tree. This is a grassland tree which has very tough roots. It takes a lot of sweat and effort to dig out the roots of that tree; men have to work till the skin comes off their fingers to do it. The use of the tree here was to express their idea of remaining strong and tough, "rooted" in their own place. They prepared various stuffs which were tough and prickly as adjuncts to their ritual: *röu* leaves, a kind of stinging ant, wild pandanus leaves, bark scrapings from the big forest trees called *kraep,* and *ui,* a prickly creeper. These things they scraped on to the pig's blood. They cut the livers into small pieces over this and made long sausages. The other meat they seasoned thoroughly too, and they prepared to dance out with fine decorations the next day. They added shreds of parsley and suet to the spices they had made. Finally they took out the special red ocher powder and rubbed it all over the livers. A big-man got up, made small piles of all this for each person, and distributed them to each man of the group. Then each man said he was eating a particular part of the man they had killed: his head, tongue, liver, kidneys, leg, arms, stomach, lower intestine, penis, testicles. They named each part of his body, including the bones, down to the last bit. Of course, they were actually only eating the pigs' livers.

When this was done, people watching from outside would see them breaking out into the open in full war display with spears and shields and would realize they had performed this ritual.[4]

These things were carried out with more intensity if a big-man was killed, and there would be a big funeral too.[5] Mourners came from group after group, wearing dried bustles at their rear, white *mara* leaves, with charcoaled bodies and carrying bundles of spears and large shields. With black bird-of-paradise plumes on their heads they made their way along the pathways. Crowds spilled one after the other into the ceremonial ground. The man's close relatives slung the dead man up on high poles out of reach, wrapped inside casuarina tree bark lined with banana leaves. The close relatives also covered themselves from head to foot in yellow mud, as if they were pigs which had been wallowing; not a part of their skin was left visible. Then they threw ashes over themselves on top of the mud. The women did the same, forming a train of mourners and performing their dance of sorrow known as *ka ökli,* the "farewell crying," festooned with weeds and cordyline leaves. The men performed charges around the outside of the women

---

[4] It was called *wuö up noromen* or *wuö kaemb kaklk noromen.*

[5] (The account that follows was true of big funerals up to 1976. An illustration of funeral behavior can be seen in part 2 of the film *Ongka's Big Moka.*)

with their spears and shields. When a new group of mourners entered, they rushed forward to greet them, the men in front with their shields, the women behind with their elaborate cordyline gear. The men stampeded, treading on people or knocking them aside if they were in the way. Pulling in the new arrivals, they led them to the central ring and crushed them in there as they charged around them. Another group appeared, arousing a fresh display, and so it continued.

At length the kin were ready to take away the body. The men divided and ran in opposite directions until they met, weaving in and out in a confused mass, in the midst of which the kin laid hold of the corpse and removed it. Two men climbed up and passed it down to four others below, who protected it from the mass of people and placed it in a men's house nearby, fastening the doorway.

Outside the mourners now sat down and orators came forward. They spoke of who had killed the man and performed the ritual of "cooking his liver," who was glad at his death, who had made hallooing noises and danced because of it. They told the visitors to tell those people that soon they would be coming out to fight over the death. It would be the only way they could ease their feelings and be elated, if they had made the attempt.

Eventually the mourners went home. The close kin first carried out the ritual called "taking *pima.*" They went out to the old cemetery, the "charcoal place," where their fathers and fathers' fathers were buried, and a senior man enumerated the pigs they were to kill, dark ones and light ones and brindled, and he announced this to the ghosts in a prayer: "We have come to your place in order to remove the front apron from our man who has died. Here are the pigs we have brought you. Our enemies are rejoicing, so now I have come to compare our man's foot with a man from among the enemies, a man who grew up at the same time, who courted girls when he did, who is of the same size and the same status. I want to kill such a man and thus be equal with them; otherwise I shall remain upset. Why have they killed my man? If they ask me for anything, I give it to them. I have not killed any of them. There is no reason for this killing. The ghost of our man who has died is still fumbling its way around;[6] its ears are deaf and its eyes are blind. You old ancestors, who died long ago, you whose eyes and ears are open, show me the way, go before me and help me so that I may kill someone and avenge his death." He called on the names of all the ghosts—his father, his father's father, his father's father's father—and asked for help. "I have wallowed in mud like a pig in my grief, I have thrown ashes on my skin. Now if I do not kill a man in revenge, they will call us women, laugh at us, point their fingers at us, and I shall be very ashamed. I have not wronged them. Why did they do this to me?" he said.

By night they burnt a piece of pork-fat over a fire, spitted on a shoot or a stick, and they watched the way the fat dripped down. If the fire burnt up brightly and the flames licked constantly at the fat until it was finished, they said, "The ghost has come to get it," but if the fire burnt low, they said, "He has not come."[7]

---

[6] (As an inexperienced ghost would.)

[7] (This was a test to see if the ghost would come and help to reveal who was truly responsible for its death.)

Next day a number of men were told to go quietly and dig the grave, lining it with leaves. This would be one of the shallow graves they made in the past, and they might be intending to take the jaw and skull and build the special house for revenge purposes, which I have described earlier. Meanwhile at the ceremonial ground people continued to bring in gifts of food for the mourners *(röng ononga),* sweet potatoes, bananas, sugarcane, and firewood; pile after pile was heaped up and presented. They said, "You will be hungry, take this food. We have no quarrel with you. Your quarrel is with your own enemies. We are your friends and we bring you food to eat here at the funeral." (Later the relatives would cook pigs to "remove the head hair" of the dead man *(peng ndi kng)* and repay these earlier gifts of food.) They saw the body would soon rot now, and the men took it off for burial.

9 / Driving Out Warfare

When we were all tired of warfare we said, "We have chased our enemies away, they have chased us away, we are all tired out now. Let us make rituals of peace by removing the *el pint pint* from our territory and cooking pigs for our allies."[1]

The first step was to place a barrier of leaves across the pathways of war, along with broken pieces of spears and shields to tell the enemy not to come and fight any more. The enemies in fact did the same. They planted cordylines, too, which would grow and stay as a sign after the other things had rotted away. They would then criticize anyone who broke the peace while they were trying to raise pigs.

Then they worked hard in their gardens and bred large herds, asking their friends for stone axes and breeding sows. They built little houses in sheltered places, keeping a male and a female pig in them, and made large numbers of sweet potato gardens all around. They made no mixed-vegetable gardens at first, only sweet potato gardens. When the sows came on heat, they swiftly put them to the boar, and so they bred successive litters and the numbers built up. The first litters grew big and old, and their teeth showed through and curled up; the next generation were big and fat too, with "water on their skins," as we say; the next ones were tied with rope and able to hold down their sweet potatoes with their feet to eat them; and the last litters were now weaned and able to smell at their sweet potato and eat it too. About three years would have gone by.

While some of the pigs were huge and fat, lounging by the doorways, others, they saw, were mangy. Garden crops, too, could be failing. When we saw this we said, "It is because of *el pint pint*.[2] Let us chase him out." Each man contributed pigs, one by one, and we gathered all kinds of greens—cucumbers, maize corn, *pit-pit*—and took them into the big communal war-house, where all the weapons were stored. This house was as large as four or even eight ordinary men's houses, and now all the men of the clan gathered inside it till they were tightly packed, body to body. Pigs were breaking into gardens, birds attacking banana fruit, crops withering, pigs getting thin: this was why we did this. We took to the war-house leaves of the *pokan, kuklumb* and *koepka* plants to be bespelled by an expert. They chose a man with long legs who was used to fooling around and dressed him up. They rubbed charcoal all over his body and then marked it further with stripes of

---

[1] *Kor nukupa kng* is the Melpa term for "cooking pigs for allies" here. For *el pint pint* see note 2.

[2] The meaning of this is that things which are *pint* are dry and hard. Charcoal, *mara* leaves, spears, and cowrie shells are all like this. So we said, "Let us get rid of all these dry things which were connected with our fighting and get back the things which are soft and make fertility instead."

white and yellow. On his face they put a gourd with two holes cut for eyepieces. As a rear covering they put old blackened cordylines on him. On his head he had a divided plume of the red bird of paradise and a tall marsupial tail, and in his hand he had an old sooty spear. He looked like some kind of crazy spirit.

They told him to lurk in the long grasses beside the gardens and then to climb a tree and hide in a crook very early in the morning without being seen by anyone. The other men came up later and proceeded to call to him up the tree:

-Who's that boy up the tree?
Is it the boy Numnumb?

He replied:

Ye-e-s.

They said:

Come down!
Quickly, quickly come down!

They repeated:

Who's that boy up there?
Is it the boy Tiktik?
Ye-e-s.
Quickly come down then!
Who's that boy up there?
Is it the boy Kundnum?
Ye-e-s.
Quickly come down then!
Who's that boy up there?
Is it the boy Pöndnum?
Ye-e-s.
Quickly come down then!

Thus they called out to the spirit figure, and then they called out to all the things that he wore or carried:

His spear of the *ndakla* kind,
His spear of the *nggoklnga* kind,
His barbed arrows,
His battle ax, *nggaema,*
His big shield,
His banana-leaf bustle,
His large cowries,
His charcoal,
His *mara*-tree sprigs,
His black cassowary plumes,
His plumes of the *kuklup* bird, the ribbon-tailed bird of paradise[3]

---

[3] (See E.T. Gilliard, *Birds of Paradise and Bower Birds,* London, 1969, p. 151 ff.)

When he had descended, they recited again all these things he had brought with him, and then said, "You brought these things, now be off with you and take them away to the valley depths of the Jimi! You have been with us too long, now go! I want to keep instead the netbags full of fresh, green, lush, soft, tender, fertile, cool things. So take all those rough things of yours off to the Jimi!"

The young men were holding clubs, and as these words were spoken, they set to and felled the pigs for sacrifice. The pigs screeched and fell down in confusion. Meanwhile the other men took up staves and addressed the spirit figure once more: "We told you to go! Why are you still here?" Bang! They took a swipe at him, and he darted away. They gave chase and pretended to fell him with their blows. He stumbled, ran, stumbled, ran, hid himself, was found, ran, hid again, ran. Across all the main pathways they pursued him until at last on the path of warfare they came to the borders with their enemies. They chased him right across this, and there they made a new ritual barrier, planting anew *pokan,* cordylines, and fragments of shields and spears. This would be near to one of the big rivers, the Ombil or Möka.

The spirit man then washed off all his soot, grime, and paint in the river water, removed his dirty clothes, washed them, and left them with his weapons beside the river. He returned to join the others in the pig-cooking. Those pigs did not die quickly but lay still writhing until they took sweet potato leaves and placed these to their noses. Then they smelled the leaves and died. The men singed and butchered the pigs and cooked also an oven-full of sweet potato tubers. When these were ready they divided them out, handing a tuber to each man or woman for each pig that they had. These were for the people to take home later and feed to their living pigs to make them healthy and grow. They said, "Now we have driven out all the bad and rough ways. Now let no man steal or insult others, let us rear our pigs to give to our allies, so that we can decorate and dance. Let all the troubles and the rough and tough ways that go with them depart, and let us take back the soft ways of friendship. In one month let us cut the firewood, in the next we shall prepare the banana leaves for the oven, in another we shall ask our friends for vegetables to help with the feast." In fact, they would be deciding on this two or three years ahead, and in each year they completed some of the preparations. They made vegetable gardens. The first was cut from wooded fallow, and the trees left standing to dry would later provide the firewood for the big cooking. The second garden was planted with the bananas whose leaves were destined for the ovens, and the third year's garden would supply the greens for the actual occasion.

Finally they cooked their pigs and called to their allies to come.[4] Before them they piled up the pork, heads, backbones, stomachs, higher and higher, and made the traditional speech: "You brought me weapons and food when I was under siege, you helped me in the fighting, you protected my women and children. For all these services I give to you all separately and in turn. Now we have made an end of this old matter and we are going to start on some new work."

---

[4] (An occasion of this kind is described in chapter 6.)

10 / My Personal Enemies

I grew up in the middle of these practices of warfare, and when the white men came we said, "These are bad ways, let's give them up, they're rubbish!"

As I have said, I was made a boss boy, then a tultul, and a luluai, and I had policemen staying with me at Mbukl to help me hear disputes and keep order. Sometimes I had difficult things to do. I was at Mbukl one day when a corporal and two constables came to me and said, "Did you know that two Minembi groups[1] have been fighting with sticks? One man, called Rona, has been killed. We want you to go with us and see about it."

I was reluctant and refused. "The Minembi will kill me. I won't go," I said. They pressed me. "You are a luluai. Come with us. We have three constables as well as a corporal." So I went with them. When we arrived, the Minembi were cooking some pigs, already making preparations to settle the matter by paying compensation for the killing with pork. But the policemen were after the actual man who had done the killing. They stayed back and told me to go in and find him. This was R., a big-man. When I went in, the Minembi were scared and said, "Here come the authorities,"[2] and they fled, leaving much of their pork already cooked and spread out near to the ovens. Those who stayed said, "What do you want? We're cooking pork." "That's all right," I said. "Where's R.?" The man was not about. We searched for him across the nearby river, but he could not be found. We waited then for four days nearby, and on the fifth day the corporal told myself and two of the police constables to go and dig up the dead man's grave and bring the remains to him. "What?" I said, "He'll be rotten by now, stinking! I won't do it. You can kill me if you like!" "It doesn't matter. Go and dig him up," he said. So I went, and with the help of several men I disinterred the corpse, and we supported it on the boards of tree bark in which it had been wrapped for burial.

The stench was very powerful; we could scarcely bear it. The corporal then told us to bind it to a pole, which we did, and next we had to carry it in the hot sun, with swarms of large blowflies buzzing around us, across to the place Krapna where R. had his house. The sun beat down on us, and the smell was sickening. When we arrived, the corporal called for R., and he, unsuspecting now, came out. The corporal ordered him to undo the vine lashings holding the thing together. "The luluai here has dug up this body," he said "and now you are to undo the vines binding it." The big-man obeyed. Then the corporal said, "Now wash it," for the flesh had rotted and fallen away from the bones. He washed it.

---

[1] These were the Numering and Nuwurung sections of the Engambo clan.
[2] (The foreigners, Kewa men, with whom Ongka as a luluai was identified.)

Now the policemen pointed to the mark of the wound in the breastbone of the skeleton and said, "Do you notice that wound? Did you see how it was made?" "I didn't see it; we were all fighting together," he replied. "Are there two of you by the same name or only one?" they asked. "No, only one. That's me." "All right, put your finger on the wound and then smell it," they said. He did so. Vomit came. "Now, then, take it and nurse it," they told him. He had to hold the rotten slimy skeleton on his knees all day from early morning when we dug it up until late afternoon. The flies buzzed round it. "Keep hold of it and keep smelling it," they said.

The people fled. "Kawelka Ongka has brought these bush spirits," they said "and ordered R. to eat up the corpse." They stayed out in the bush for three or four nights. After this was over, the police took the big-man and five other men who had started the fighting and jailed them in Hagen. All the tribes were busy at war in those times, like a red bird of paradise that argues that it will outlast the tree on which it displays, but when they heard of this event, how Ongka had dug up a corpse, a thing of disgust, and the Minembi big-man had been forced to nurse it on his lap, then they dropped all that business of fighting. "Don't let us fool around any more with warfare," they said.

Later I had to do the same kind of thing again, this time down in the Jimi Valley. A man of Tipuka Wanyembo clan had killed his wife, an Oklembo woman. She had come to his men's house where her husband was talking with some guests and started an argument with him. He told her to leave, but she refused, and in anger he reached for a long piece of cassava root intending to give her a smack with it. She turned her face away and somehow the root pierced her neck like a spear and she died of it. Corporal Tilaka said, "Kawelka Ongka will go down there and dig her up." It was in the low-lying and hot Jimi area, where things rot fast.

I didn't want to go and claimed I had been sick for a day and was unfit, but they said that I was the only man who could handle the job, and so I went again. At Kotna, in the valley to the east of Mbukl, we met a party of men accompanying the Chimbu police constable called Muli. I protested and claimed again to be sick. "If you're sick, we'll go and fetch some medicine for you," they suggested. "All right, never mind, I'm not sick yet, I just thought I might be going to get sick. Let's go," I replied.

The husband's two brothers were at his place when we got there, and I asked them to dig into the grave from some way to the side, so that they could get at the corpse which in the hot climate would certainly have rotted. As they dug close to it, such a stench arose we could not stay near it. I crushed some foul-smelling leaves of the *ndulkina* plant and pushed them through my nose,[3] so that their smell went into my nose and eyes and I did not feel the corpse's stink. I took a bamboo knife and cut away the flesh, following the policemen's instructions. All the other parts of the body were rotted pale, but the place where the wound had been inflicted was dark and swollen up with contused blood. That was where the root had entered and broken through her lower jaw into her neck. "Oh!" we said. Then we had to wrap the corpse, sling it to a pole, and carry it all the way to

---

[3] (Ongka's septum is pierced, to allow insertion of conus shell and other ornaments at times of dancing.)

Hagen,[4] up the mountainside pass and then over the hills to the government station. The white man[5] saw us and asked, "Who dug her up?" "It was Ongka." "Oh, the man we've heard about from down that way," he said. He told me to come back in a week's time and then he gave me a reward of five pounds.

Although warfare was now stopped, my own life was put in danger by something that happened. It had to do with Nggaep, the eldest son of the big-man Kitepi Kuri. We both courted the same girl, called Kope of the Eltimbo clan. She liked us both and to each of us she spoke of marriage. However, I let Nggaep marry her and in fact I helped him with his bride-wealth payment by contributing some pearl shells, pigs, and a cassowary to it. He had three other wives already and I had only one, but I let him take her.

The next thing was that he didn't take her into his own household[6] but left her to stay with her own people, and disappointed by this she came and made eyes at me again. "He seduced me and married me," she said, "but now he doesn't want me and doesn't look after me. He sleeps with some of his wives even in his own men's houses, but he's cast me out. Now I want to marry you." "What?" I replied. "That would be all right if you were still unmarried, but you're not. The man's my relative, you'll get me into trouble with this talk, so the answer is no." She insisted. "He's got three or four other wives and he isn't interested in me. I want you." So I had intercourse with her and we began to meet secretly. I realized this was dangerous and actually went to tell Nggaep. "Look, this woman spoke of marrying me as well as you, Now you've married her, but you're not looking after her and she's making eyes at me again, so take her into your own settlement place." Nggaep said, "Let her sleep where she likes. Carry on looking after her as you wish," and he went off. However, afterwards he went quietly to her and said, "I hear you're making eyes at Ongka. I'll kill you and throw you into the bushes." Afraid, she said, "No, don't kill me. It was he who enticed me and has had intercourse with me." "All right, I won't kill you. You go to him and say you want to kill me so you will be free to marry him and ask him to give you some sorcery stuff to kill me with." So she came over to me and said all this. "What? He's my nephew, my sister's son. I can't do it. Sex with you is all right, but killing him is not. You clear off," I told her. "No, give me some sorcery stuff," she said. "If you don't I'll take you to court." "Okay, we can go to court and you'll get in jail too," I said. We argued up and down and she went away.

She found some old trade salt[7] and took it to her husband, claiming it was sorcery stuff I had given her to kill him. Later, when the government officer came to visit us, he brought this out and showed it to him, saying I had tried to kill him with it. I replied that I had told both the officer and him about the problem over this woman long ago and he had done nothing about it, so why was he trying to court me about it now? This was true, and the officer agreed and said he would not hold a court to hear this matter.

---

[4] (A distance of at least 30 miles.)

[5] (Government officer.)

[6] (Doubtless this was already quite full.)

[7] This was of a kind white men don't carry around now, but the early missionaries used to have it; it was rather tasteless.

In front of everyone I then took hold of the stuff which was supposed to be sorcery-stuff or poison[8]—indeed it was poison, for they had mixed it with their own store of lethal stuff—and I said, "Let's try it out, then." I made a prayer to the ghosts. "If I have tried to kill Nggaep with this, then let me eat it all myself now and die. But if he is accusing me falsely, may I eat it and live. Instead, he will die." I thought "Let me die, then, if I have to. Let us see whether the ghosts will help me or not." I tipped the whole lot into my mouth and ate it.

My clansmen set up a wail, thinking I was doomed. However, I waited for two nights and nothing happened, so they said I had truly won. Two months went by. Nggaep was suddenly taken sick and in three days he was dead. The Tipuka, his tribesmen, thought I had secretly killed him, but I replied, "Who would have taken poison from my hand and given it to him? I have not been near him or touched him." However, they still thought I had done it by some trick and they determined to kill me.

Everyone came to his funeral. Nggaep was a big-man, son of a big-man. Our enemies, the Minembi, danced and sang with joy, performed the rite of "eating his liver," and hallooed with delight, claiming the death was caused by their own sorcery. Nevertheless, the Tipuka said it was I who had done it and invited everyone of their tribe to join in trying to kill me. The other Kawelka men left my settlement place in fear, and I was left to my own devices at Mbukl. Men waited outside my house with spears at the ready. I was forced to live in lavatories, menstrual huts,[9] pig nests. They scanned the pathways and reported me as seen coming up the hill at Nunga in Tipuka territory, and there they waited to ambush me, weapons poised, eyes watching. But somehow I gave them the slip, and they said I had passed through looking like a woman or a small child. Tired of setting ambushes, they tried poisoning me. They tipped poison into our drinking tubes, but these broke before my lips touched them. They offered me sweet potatoes, which I refused. They inserted poison into corncobs outside my house, but I detected it and threw all the corn away. They put poisoned rats into traps of mine, so I would think they had been caught fresh there, but I recognized this and discarded them.

Once five men[10] of Kitepi clan all came and surrounded my lavatory house before dawn, expecting me to come out and use it. Early that morning I slipped out, my ax tucked in my belt, to join the other men in a men's house a little way off. The enemies' spears were all around me, but they must have thought I was a cloud or some mist or else a fog really did come down and obscure the view. Anyhow I passed through. They waited and waited. Eventually they thought I must have hidden down the lavatory hole. One of them rushed into it and plunged his spear into the hole, expecting to hear me yell. Instead all he heard was a plop and a splash, and he withdrew his spear covered in muck. I was back inside my own house by then, and I heard it all happen outside.

---

[8] (The Hagen idea is that there are lethal substances that can kill people if ingested in food or drink. Sometimes these may be bespelled to make them more powerful. As a translation term "poison" conveys the idea of lethal substance, and "sorcery stuff" the idea of bespelling it.)

[9] (These are used by women during the time of their periods. Men ordinarily would never go into them for fear of danger to their bodies.)

[10] (Names omitted.)

Another time they told me a white man had asked me to join him in the Jimi Valley on a patrol and I was to go there. They had detailed some Jimi men off to kill me if I went. However, I said I didn't know that particular white man and wouldn't go. Finally two men[11] of Tipuka gave some poison stuff to a Kawelka woman who was married to a police constable stationed at Mbukl,[12] and told her to tip some of it into a cigarette for me. She, however, brought the stuff straight up to me and told me the story. "All right," I said, and had the policeman call the two men up to Mbukl.

I strapped them tightly, standing upright, and told them to reveal their penises and pull the foreskins back. Whack! I caned them till the blood and urine fell down. I had told everyone from around to come and watch, and a big crowd was there. As I beat the two of them, they trampled one another in fear to get away. Then I showed one of the two men the piece of cigarette and suggested he eat it. He refused, and I asked him why: had he planned to kill me? He admitted it. "Why did you do that?" I demanded. "I held the bone of Nggaep,"[13] he said. "What do you mean? Did you find the poison I used or did you find my footsteps round his body?" "No, I was asked to do it." "Who asked you?" "It was Kitepi so-and-so" (naming him).

All right. I took the poisoned tobacco and told him to eat it. I forced his mouth open and pushed it down. I beat him until my cane splintered. I seized the man he had named, bound him, and beat him too till the blood ran, and the crowd scattered again like wild pigs, treading on one another in their confusion. Those men lay there overnight, and the next day I extracted two large fat pigs from them. These I cooked and distributed the meat to everyone. Then I told the people, "You have seen everything now. Men cover up their fronts with aprons and their rears with bustles of leaves, but now I've stripped these two men. You have seen their penises and anuses, and they have been made very ashamed for their secret attempt to kill me. Now I have taken two of their pigs and cooked them. If ever anyone comes up here again and tries to do anything to me, I'll do something else to them, and all of you can come up here and watch again. It is God on high who knows whether I have done any wrong or not, and if I have it is he who will kill me for it. I have stripped and beaten these two men and taken their pigs. All this you have seen. Now go." The crowd heard and dispersed. In those days I used to look fiercely at people. I carried my sharp ax and my long spear, and when I met people near my place I asked them, "Where do you think you're going and why?" They would shy off and say, "Just over there to visit." They sometimes urinated where they stood in fear of what I might do to them.

After this incident my enemies were puzzled and didn't know what to do. However, an Oklembo man[14] who was my own in-law (brother of the first wife I had married and also husband to one of our own clanswomen) made a plan to finish me off. He invited me down to his place, giving me to understand he had some pearl shells for me. I went down to see. He told me, "Come again tomorrow, the

---

[11] (Names omitted.)

[12] (This was one of the women Ongka mentioned earlier as among his old courting partners.)

[13] (He held a relic of Nggaep's and intended to avenge him.)

[14] (Name omitted.)

shells aren't quite ready yet." He kept putting me off and I trudged up and down the hill between my place and his until two weeks had gone by and I was tired of it. I decided he was planning to kill me, so I began to take three of our own men down with me.[15] They hid themselves in an old sugarcane and banana garden nearby, eating little bits of cane and waiting for me to call out to them in case of trouble.

More weeks went by with visits like this. He kept setting and resetting the shells in their resin backings.[16] He said he had eight ready but wanted to make up a set of ten for me, in return for the big pig I had previously given him. I said it didn't matter, but he insisted. One day I went down and saw that he had with him four other men,[17] one of whom had a name for killing people either with the ax or with poison. I thought, "This is it, they're going to kill me now, openly." I kept a close watch on either side of me as I sat among them.

We stayed there without saying much. Then finally he said, "It's hot. Let's cook ourselves some greens from my new garden." This was a little vegetable garden near to his new men's house. He took heated stones and made a little oven near to the center post of the house, while I observed him with care. He went inside his sleeping-place, partitioned off at the back of the house, came out, went in again, hemmed and hawed, and scrabbled on the floor. "What are you after?" I thought, not letting my eyes off him. (I'm short-sighted now, but I had keen eyes then.) "I'm looking for a smoke I've dropped," he mumbled. He didn't know what to do with himself in his nervousness. I decided to let him get on with it and said I was going outside for a breath of air and to get myself a leaf to roll some tobacco in.[18] While I was outside he swiftly removed the greens from the oven and divided them into portions for each one of us. He tipped poison like so much salt into my portion, mixed it in thoroughly, and then seasoned it with some more on top. I pretended to be aware of nothing as I reentered the house and sat down, but I had my sharp ax with me.

I said, "I don't like this type of greens, they make me feel nauseous, so I don't eat them." "What? But it's hot and we've cooked them specially for you to refresh yourself with! Do have some!" they said. "No, thank you, I'm afraid it makes me sick, but do carry on and enjoy it yourselves." I settled myself down firmly with my ax slung over my shoulder and looked at them. Slowly each man turned to his own portion and ate it, leaving mine sitting there untasted. The other men went outside one by one until only I and my would-be poisoner were left together. I whistled, scratched my back with the ax handle, shifted the position of my legs, and said, "Why have your guests left so quickly without eating much? Are you going to eat all those greens by yourself?" He made no reply but was ill at ease and fiddled with things on the floor. "Do eat it yourself, then," I said, staring at

---

[15] These were Tiki, Pena, and Pundukl.
[16] (The pearl shells were set into backings of resin obtained from the *kilt* and *elua* trees. To soften the resin, stones were heated and applied to shape the resin around the shell itself.)
[17] (Names omitted.)
[18] (The *neng* plant grows in hedgerows and supplies a leaf which can be used for this purpose. It is also the sacred divination substance of the Tipuka tribe, by which they swear that they have done no evil, as an ordeal. As these Tipuka men were trying to kill him, Ongka's remark here may possibly have carried a deeper message.)

him. "Or are you going to call your sons in to finish it off? Perhaps the others will be returning?" He was thoroughly discomfited and at last broke down.

"Oh," he said, "I've been trying to kill you,[19] but you've found me out." "What?" I said, "I'm not wounded." "No, by poison." "Oh. Where is the container in which you stored the poison, then? If you don't show that to me, I'll say it's just a lie and make you eat those greens while I stand here and watch you." He scratched his head for nonexistent lice. "My brother-in-law, it's true," he said, and reached for the vial of poison which was inside his sleeping room. It was a little bamboo tube stoppered with gray marsupial fur. "Here," he said, and lifted the stopper for me to look inside. There were multicolored fine grains lying there, some glistening, some black. It was poison all right. "Don't kill me, I'll do some-thing," he said, and brought out two beautiful pearl shells, full of luster, which others had given him as an encouragement to kill me. "That's not enough," I said. "That's just what you owe me for the pig I gave you." I had my ax at the ready still. He went out and pulled in a huge fat sow with firm gleaming sides and tied it to a stake. "Good," I said.

I called to Pundukl, Tiki, and Pena. One I told to take the shells and the other two to truss up the pig and prepare to take it off up the hill, while I guarded them with my ax. "If you're attacked on the way," I said, "we'll drop these things and I'll kill one or two of them before we retreat to Mbukl." Then we went for home, and who would challenge us once we reached our own garden areas? At Mbukl, people say, there's a wild dog that guards the place.[20]

The man who wanted to kill me still would not forget. While I slept in my own house, I was in danger every night, so I made myself a cave. I dug up an area inside thick stands of cane-grass, covered the top with slats and placed tussocks and cane-grass on top of it again. I made a tunnel into it from the side and covered the entrance way with banana leaves. I had a blanket and dried leaves inside the place on which I used to sleep. It was beside the pathway to the lavatory where no one walks. Every night I slept in there with my weapons at my side and slipped out in the early morning.

However, one night when heavy rain was pouring down, a man of our own clan, who had turned to helping his mother's people among the Tipuka, spied on me by hiding himself inside the women's lavatory. This was the kind of thing that bad rubbish men, who are swayed by bribes, do. Good men of one's own group would not do a thing like that. But even with his help they could not kill me. I played no tricks with magic or witchcraft; it was God alone who helped me. As a matter of fact I don't believe in the tricks of magic. I believe only that we have some dreams which are proved true.

He watched me as I came along in the downpour and saw how I placed my foot on a log and sprang into the undergrowth. Then he went to tell his friends, the same ones who had surrounded my lavatory place earlier. In the daytime he re-turned and saw everything, and at night four of them returned to ambush me. I ar-rived, waving a burning stick in the rain and darkness, and went inside to sleep. I

[19] (Literally, "I've been trying to cook your blood," that is, make it dry.)
[20] (Meaning Ongka himself.)

had earlier made a second entrance tunnel leading down to a pigs' pathway, although I had not used it and it was covered by grasses. This was the only bit they had not seen. Rain thudded down and I dozed off, but quickly woke when I heard something snap up above me. "Probably pigs moving about," I thought. Then something fastened itself to my leg and pinched me. Was it an insect, or a ghost warning me? "Perhaps someone's after me," I thought. I folded my blankets in a pile. Fully awake, with my bow and arrow in one hand and my ax in the other, I crept out along the secret second tunnel and into the open. Although heavy rain was falling, as I poked my head out it was light enough at ground level to see a little, and I noticed shadowy figures moving around. "Oh," I thought.

I went back in and made some loud snoring noises so they would think I was asleep, then crept out again very quietly, thinking all the time they would see or hear me. I stole round to the back of a woman's house, which was not far off, and settled myself into a pile of rubbish which was used for topping up earth ovens. They waited until they thought I was fully asleep, then they broke into my hideout and thrust their spears through empty blankets. They were taken aback. "What? Is he a ghost or a witch? We tried to get him in his lavatory before, and our spears drove into the muck. We tried to poison him, and he stripped our men, beat their penises till blood flowed, and took our pigs to cook and eat along with the policemen. We tried to poison him again, and he took our fat pig and shells. Now this. Let's give up. He's impossible!" they said.

These men are all still alive and live near here; they are well known to us all. When they look at me they know they tried to kill me and I escaped, and they wonder if I'm some kind of spirit. They tried to kill me secretly, they tried to kill me openly, but they failed, and here I still am.

11 / Wind Work

Recently some men set up the business called "wind work." They spoke of a man named Makla of Kiklpukla tribe down at Tiki, saying that he had thousands and thousands of dollars in box after box after box.[1]

Makla's followers used to display the keys to these boxes, strung in long chains round their necks like decorations. As contributions to support the cultists and their leader Makla, and in hope of vast returns, people brought in countless gifts of pigs, chickens, freezer meat purchased from stores, carton after carton of Gold Leaf cigarettes; the shops were emptied of their goods. I said, "All right, that's good. Now, have you seen the money?" "Yes, we've seen it," they said. "Be careful not to tell lies," I told them. "I've slept outside in cemetery places to see if spirits would come there, but I didn't see any. People think they hear spirits talking, but it's birds whistling or marsupials scuffling about. So don't lie about it." "What? Listen! It's true! We have seen it," they said. All the important men in our Dei Council area said the same thing. One of the Ndika tribe's leaders, who lives just behind the Lutheran mission at Ogelbeng, he had his boxes and keys too. Councilors of the Römndi and Minembi, they had theirs. In fact, I was the only one who was against it, I, a rubbish-man against all the big-men. Some said that I had escaped death many times from poison and ambush and that I spoke the truth, but they scoffed and replied that I had been right in the past but was wrong now.

"All right," I said. "Let's see what they can produce." The leader of the cult, Makla, married four wives on the strength of his money, all daughters of big-men. "Forget about your coffee gardens, your pigs, and your business," he told people. "There's so much money here for you, you won't be able to finish spending it no matter how you try. The ghosts have brought us a huge store of money." One woman, a leader in the cult, declared that she had made at her husband's place a "Commonwealth Bank" and a "Development Bank" and a new bank of her own creation, the "Kiluwa bank,"[2] and that these were all crammed full of money boxes. She and her husband and a company of supporters even came down to the capital city, Port Moresby, on a plane journey to the coast in search of the secrets to wealth. Their followers raised money for them, $10 for each box they had, until about $400 to $500 were raised.

---

[1] (Makla was the leader of the "red box" money cult, which began in Dei Council in the late 1960s and flourished in the early 1970s. "Wind work," or *köpkö kongon,* was so called because the ghosts who were to supply the money were said to be able to send messages and travel on the wind.)

[2] (The first two were names of banks established in Papua New Guinea. The third appears to be named after the impressive mountain southwest of Mount Hagen, which appears on maps as Mount Giluwe.)

So they bought air tickets and came down to Port Moresby, saying some spirits had arrived there and they wanted to talk to them. The woman cult leader bought herself a long wig made of white women's hair and a pair of dark glasses. She put these on and claimed she was the Queen, and people saw the wig, without knowing of such things or how she got it, and were taken aback. "It's true, she's become a queen!" they exclaimed. They were all sleeping together in a little house occupied by another Hagener working in Port Moresby, and one night they were in there holding a seance when a young Hagen ne'er-do-well about town came up to the doorway, a bit tipsy, and asked what they were up to. "Sh! We're talking to the spirits!" they said, and wouldn't let him in. Annoyed, he broke the door down and let fly at them with his feet. They ran outside, exclaiming in alarm that the spirits had all been frightened away, and what would they do now? There they stayed outside till dawn came.

As a climax to their cult they staged a big dance and called for pigs to be brought in as final contributions. In return for a single pig they were promising they would give back about $10 million. For each pig, note. Well, people from all the groups around brought in pigs. "There's so much money, you'll leave some lying there," the woman cult leader said. I felt sure this was all lies and simply a means to consume all the gifts that were being brought in. They got hold of a car belonging to one of our clansmen, who was married into their group, and he carted boxes around for them day and night. In opposition to all this, I put up a wager. I bet my big pig, called Rut Pepa,[3] and fifty dollars in cash, against a pig of theirs, saying that if they got the money they could eat my pig, but if not I would eat theirs. They laughed and said, "You poor fool! We'll soon be down to eat that pig of yours, so be ready."

They prepared their big dance. Oh, the long dark plumes of their headdresses, all waving in the sun! I thought, "My old male pig I've kept for so many years, does this mean they're really going to get it?" One of the government officers came to see me and I said to him, "All the councilors and the big-men are saying they'll be cooking my pig. Do you think it's true?" "No, you did well to make your bet," he replied. "I'll bet some money along with yours, so you won't be the only one to lose," he added. "Then we'll see," he remarked. "I'm not going to interfere at all, but you go up there and just say a few words." Andrew[4] was there too and he was cautious. "No, don't say anything if you go. They're very worked up and intent on this. Just let them get on with it," he suggested. The government officer said, "All right, I'll just put my bet in along with Ongka, and we can go up and have a look." He came behind, and Andrew and I went up first.

I found their group in full dance array; the women's necks were festooned tightly up to their ears with keys to the cult boxes. When I asked them, though, if the boxes would be opened that day, they said no, it was just dancing today. All right. I had brought my dog. Its real name was Bikbel ("big stomach"), but I gave it a slightly different name that day, thinking of how the cultists had received and

---

[3] (This was one of those that Ongka later gave away in moka in 1974. See the end of chapter 7 and also chapter 13.)

[4] (One of the authors.)

"eaten" all the things people had brought to them. So I called, "Where's my dog gone? My dog, Eat-All! Eat-All! Eat-All! Where are you?" One of the big-men of Minembi,[5] who had brought in a long bamboo full of decorating oil as a present for them, said, "What sort of a name is that for a dog?" I said, "It's my dog that I brought here from a distant place. It's got lost in the crowd. Come and help me find it. Eat-All! Eat-All! Come here!" When the dog came to me, I said, "Eat-All, you bad dog! Have you been eating pigs' bones about the place? You'll make yourself sick!"

They didn't bring out the money that day, or the next; many days went by with no result and they kept saying, "Tomorrow." One of the cultists had taken to himself two new wives, young girls both called Mone, and he had given them his boxes, saying that he would later bring them the keys, open the boxes, and pay bride-wealth for them with the money. He sent the boxes off with the girls' kinsfolk in fact. Those boxes were heavy and they thought they were full of treasure. But he didn't bring them the keys. Eventually they grew tired of waiting and said, "He's got our girls, let's get the cash." So they broke open the boxes. They found old bits of scrap metal thrown away by white men, some old radio batteries, and quantities of ordinary river stones. In disgust they tipped it all out, then went and took back their women.

They had all lost. Everyone asked me, "How did you know? Who taught you?" "No one taught me. I thought it out for myself.[6] My father and grandfather told me no tales of this kind. I never heard of spirits actually coming and eating up pork and bones as they said they were doing in this cult.[7] People talk of spirits, but I find it's birds or marsupials. White men, it is true, have brought strong things to us; they can fly through the air and speed across land and water. But as for ourselves, we lie and trick; these things are not true." Oh, those people now, when I see them walking along the road in the hot sun as I go past in my car, I say to them, "Hello, you're the people who made money by wind work, you must be rich. Can I work as your laborer and build your lavatory or dig your rubbish tip for you?" "Oh, Ongka, you're biting us and eating us up!" they say in despair and shame. Then I give them a ride,[8] charging them a fare of course, and they pay up quickly in case I should say anything more. The people who ran the cult don't walk about much in public any more.

Makla started this, and it was taken up by everyone, all the tribes around. It spread like wildfire.[9] When the thing collapsed, Makla was put in jail[10] and his wives left him and married other men. The various cult-places were broken down, their fences destroyed, and the houses left to rot.

---

[5] Nindi of Papeke clan.

[6] (I had discussed the cult with Ongka, of course, but had striven to take a stance on it that was uncommitted either way. But I did not support it, and perhaps my actions were taken by him as the more reliable guide—Andrew Strathern.)

[7] (The cult operators may have secured food supplies for themselves in this way.)

[8] (At one stage of the cult, the operators declared they were about to purchase a ten-ton truck with cult money. One was actually delivered, but removed when no money was forthcoming.)

[9] Kombukla, Ukini, Maplke, Palke, Minembi, and Kawelka men took it up. (The list is not exhaustive.)

[10] (This was on a charge of spreading false rumors.)

12 / The Jimi Valley

I have spent a good deal of my time down in the Jimi Valley. Down there, there are many different kinds of products: special types of cane, nuts, fruits, cassowaries, wild pigs, snakes, lizards, and fish. Back in our own place, which we call *Korka kona,* we do not have so many good foods. Our taro and yams are small because our ground is rather dry, but all the foods in the Jimi grow to a large size.

The pathways into this area are steep; the hills stand up in rows before you. You take your wives and children and walk in front, slashing the overhanging growth away, up into the dripping, slippery mountain moss, then on the other side you head down a sheer slope, down, down, down, to the banks of the big Muglpin River. We used to cross this on makeshift bridges of sticks and small trees strung together by vines. Each time we crossed, the men had to relash the bridge and then help across their wives and children who would be carrying greens, pork, or pandanus fruit. Over on the other side was the territory of the groups which properly belong to the Jimi—the Palke, Maplke, and Romalke—and beyond these again, mostly on the northern side of the large Jimi River itself, there are people with a different language. At the western lower end of this big river are the Epi and Kurup groups, while near our own southern side there are sections of Klamakae and Tipuka groups which have migrated down there.

The Palke have an old origin place which is quite near to Mbukl, but both they and the Maplke have lived down in the Jimi for a long time. There is a story that there were two brothers on the far side of the Jimi river, and they quarreled over the rights to a vegetable garden. The one told the other to leave, and he went off with a little pig, a bow, and arrows and came up to a place called Pintpint. There a snake came and ate up his pig, disappearing into a cave nearby. Fearing that the snake would eat him too, he left and walked on and on till he came to the place Ombin. There a man of Epilke tribe had made a garden. As he was hungry he picked a banana at the edge of the garden, and as he did so the garden owner came by and saw him. The owner looked at him carefully, then showed him another bunch, and watched as he peeled and ate these. He gave him sugarcane. The newcomer laid its peel in a pile as ordinary men do and ate the cane. The Epilke man accepted him as a human being, and, telling him to stay in the garden, he went back home. There he told his unmarried sister to go and have a look at the man and see what he was doing. There he was, still quietly eating. So the man told his sister to stay with the stranger and be his wife, and as bride-wealth the newcomer handed over the only thing he had, his bow and arrows. The woman bore a son called Komon ("the elder") and another called Atek ("the younger"), and finally one called Ökl (from the name of the stream beside which he was born).

These were the original ancestors of the subgroups of Maplke tribe. Since then Epilke and Maplke have fought in warfare, and in their ceremonial speeches the Epilke say it was the arrows the first Maplke man handed over to them in bride-wealth that enabled them to fight and beat them in warfare. So that was how the Maplke originated, in the Jimi area itself.

The Jimi people trap animals. They make a hole in the ground, cover it with camouflage, and fence it off. Slats of wood are stuck in it, protruding through the top, and on these they impale nuts, which the animals come to smell and so tumble headlong into the hole. A hunter may prepare eight or ten traps like this and would be delighted if he found wild pigs in perhaps half of them. Then he calls his people to come into the big forest, and they arrive with those special *uya* nuts, which they chew up and spit on the pig's blood and fat to make tasty sausages. They bring their own salt and bananas, and they steam-cook the flesh. Their menfolk may stay out for two weeks in the forest, sleeping in rough shelters, before they succeed in catching enough wild pigs. When they finally cook them they add to the ovens all manner of foods, marsupials, brush turkeyeggs,[1] nuts, and lizards. When those *uya* nuts are in season, they use them as bait. When they are not, they look for steep hillsides where the pigs find it difficult to climb up and they fence off the hill, laying the trap down below where the animal will find an easy way through. When the *uya* nuts are available, they actually make the traps right at the foot of the nut tree, and as the pig comes rooting along it either tumbles in head first or crashes through the struts on which the camouflage is placed. After they have captured the pigs, men take their axes and make a drumming noise with the butts on the prominent roots of a tree, thus calling their friends to come and help. If their families have traveled out to the shelter houses, some of them stay back to prepare materials for the ovens. When the meat is carried in, they give it a first steaming in an oven above ground surrounded by slabs of wood. Then they place the meat on trestles, remove the bones, sort it, and put it back into an ordinary oven for the final steaming. The heads of wild pigs are tough but very tasty if cooked properly, and these they steam in a separate oven with taro and yams. The oven for these heads is made deep and narrow. It is covered with earth and the meat left for many hours; if it is placed in the oven in early morning, it will not be removed until evening time.

The rest of the food is cooked more quickly and laid on trestles in the shelter house, and the men go out with dogs just before dawn to search for more animals and birds that feed at night and look for resting places in these early hours of day. As they shoot more animals, these are collected and cooked too, and salted to make them keep. It may be four days before they finally grow tired and take all their meat home with them.

Another time they go out to catch fish. They make fish traps from tough tree bark.[2] They close these at one end and make a spring catch baited with a grub inside a rolled-up length of bark. They lay numbers of these traps in big pools where

---

[1] The brush turkey lays a clutch of anything from five to thirty-two eggs and covers these with successive mounds of rubbish to incubate them. Men then rifle the mounds for the eggs. They shoot the adult bird too.

[2] From the *mömin* and *kopon wantep* trees.

they have observed fish, weighting them down with stones to keep them in place. It takes a single man a week to make between five and fifteen of these traps, for they have to be sewn and lashed together with care. The fish see the grub bait and swim inside; then the door is sprung and they are caught. They settle down quietly, and the hunter finds them in the early morning when he checks his traps. Sometimes they make an extra-large trap, sewn with cane, the holes pierced with a cassowary bone, and into this they transfer all the catches from the smaller traps. The fish lie there quietly for weeks or months and don't seem to lose condition, even though they are in captivity and can't eat all their usual foods. The hunters put dozens and dozens of fish in these big store-traps.

They observe certain taboos with great care during this time. A man must not have intercourse with his wife, he must not eat red pandanus fruit, he must not eat hibiscus leaves *(kim weka)* or steamed sweet potato, nor must he tread on pig muck. He tells people that he is hunting for marsupials but hasn't found any yet. They realize and think, "Oh, he's got some fish." He won't eat pork from a pig that has died of sickness, and he doesn't oil his body with pig fat. Some of these things are avoided because they are slippery, and so he thinks that the fish will escape, others because they create a smell which would frighten off the fish, and others because if he ate them the fish would die in the big trap.

After perhaps two months of hunting, the men decide to steam-cook the fish, so they carry the traps home, empty the fish out onto leaves, and stun each one with a blow from a stick. They wrap them in soft furry *menaplka* leaves and hang them up in a display. In the Jimi area such fish can be used as gifts in ceremonial exchanges. They may cook them along with some pork, laying the pork in the oven first. They distribute them to the men who looked after their gardens while they were out hunting, who staked their sugarcanes, or who propped up and wrapped their bunches of bananas to make them ripen, for these are two tasks which they themselves must not do. Each man who helped gets two fish and all help willingly with the work of cooking.

Another way they catch fish is by damming streams. They find a place where there is an island in a river, around which the river divides into two channels, and they select one of these channels for damming at both ends. First they lay big logs across the center of the stream, and these they support by piles driven in right from one bank to the other. They do this at both ends of the island. When dry weather comes and the level of the stream begins to fall, they cut large sections of strong tree bark and lay these successively across the dam, weighting them with stones and making them overlap so that no holes are left. Any little interstices remaining are stuffed with leaves. Then they bring slabs of sticky, muddy earth and smear these over the bark at the top to complete the dam. Now the mud and bark form a solid obstacle and most of the water is diverted round to the other channel. The men prepare sticks and beds of leaves at the bottom end of the dammed-up area. As the water dries up, the fish all swim down to this end and begin to flip and twist as the pools become more and more shallow and muddy. Now is the time to kill them. Men close in, striking them with sticks. The really long fish[3]

[3] (Eels.)

have to be speared, for they will even bite people if they move onto dry land. In one day a great many fish can be killed by this method.

The kinds of fish found are numerous: *kaema, koep, pil, ndembal, nomung, kan,* and *korloma. Kaema* is medium-sized, about a foot and a half long. *Ndembal* is small, with gray-green markings on its back. *Nomung* has dark blue markings. *Korloma* has a short body with a large head and an especially prominent bony brow. When they cook it, its meat is strong and sweet, like that of a pig's backbone.

There is a story about the head of the *korloma* fish. When men want landslides to occur in the territory of an enemy, they take a head of this fish and hide it way up at the headwaters of a feeder stream. The fish itself they catch in a big river much further down-valley, and they tell the river. "Now we are taking your strong thing away from you and are going to bury it up in that stream." They take some pebbles and stones from the bed of the big river too. So the river hears this, and they take the fish and the stones and bury them as they say. The head of this fish, by the way, also has two places in which there are stones, which make it strong and heavy. The men break off pieces of casuarina, bark and wood from trees near to where they have buried the head, and they take these back and show them to the big river, saying, "We give these to you, so go now."

The big river now asks the streams that flow into it, "Where do you come from?" When he finds one that starts from where the *korloma* head is buried, he says, "Quickly now, go and get that strong thing of mine which is buried up there and bring it back to me." The little stream hears and obeys. It tears at its banks, heavy rain falls, and landslides occur as it tries to reach the fish's head buried at its own top end.

There are plenty of cassowaries in the Jimi too. They eat the fruits of trees[4] and defecate these out on the spot. Men find their feeding places and set up snares. A cassowary comes, smelling its way forward to the fruits, and its head is caught in the snare. It twists and turns and tears at itself to escape. The men may even bait the place with their own excrement, for the cassowary likes everything that is rotten. So they make a fence, then they defecate inside this and set up a snare just above the spot. The cassowary comes running by, smells it, turns aside to investigate, and pokes its head further and further forward until the snare seizes it. It thrashes wildly around and may smash its own jaw. They take it home, grumbling about working in their own stench, and cook it.

We hunt other birds up in the trees, constructing ladders to help us climb into the really big ones and find their nests in holes or forks of branches.[5] To catch eagles we have to use a wickerwork basket. Men find where the eagle's nest is, high up in a huge tree, made of sticks, and they suspend this basket above it from a branch by long vines that stretch right down to the ground. The eagle flies around catching its prey, and eventually it returns and settles on its nest. The men watch and pull smartly on the vines. Down comes the basket over the nest and the eagle flaps vainly to get free. While one man holds tightly to the vines, another climbs the tree up to the nest, lets the eagle get as much as its head out, then strikes it

---

[4] These are the *woti, menaplka, kopil,* and *kama* trees.
[5] In this way we catch *puklör, konmba* (cockatoo), *korlop* (hornbill), and *kondopakl.*

1975. At his old settlement place at Mbukl, Ongka makes an invocation to spirits of his own sub-clan in pairs, calling to them to ensure his continuing good luck in exchange, hunting (especially in the Jimi Valley) and in avoiding death at the hands of his enemies. Sacrificial items, including a used gun cartridge carton and a cassowary claw, are about to be thrown into a fire as offerings.

1975. Ongka butchers a pig killed as a sacrifice for this occasion.

senseless. Pairs of eagles, male and female, may be taken in this way. When the first one is taken, the hunter quickly rearranges the eggs, placing their good side up if they have been cracked. Soon the mate comes, hoo-hooing in the forest; it thinks its mate will be back later and it lands, and so it is captured too.

The hornbill has a sharp beak, so they fill up its hole with the aid of a stick from a distance before going in to take it. Then they seize its neck and strike it with the stick.

We catch the white bird of paradise too, the bird which is on all the pictures nowadays.[6] This is a bird that dances. It swings on a branch from side to side, upside down, right way up, cawing to itself. When it stops you might think it was dead, then it sways up to its next position. Several of them, up to eight or sixteen, may perform on the same tree, the plumaged birds dancing in front of the ones without plumage, which fly around watching and admiring. Men observe all this and make a little house with a floor near the place where the birds dance. They can tell the place because with the birds' clawing and swinging movements the bark is stripped off and the wood gleams white. They support the house with strong vines and camouflage it with bundles of dried fruit pandanus leaves so that it is dark inside. Then they take the bole of a palm tree and hollow its soft center out and line it up with the birds' dancing place. The birds dance only in the early morning and the evening, and the man builds his hut during the day while they fly off in search of water and fruits.

The birds come back and notice the house. They think, "This is something new here" and for two or three days they avoid the place. Later they see it is still there and they think, "This thing is here to stay, so it doesn't matter," so they come clawing and hanging around it again. The hunter meanwhile sleeps in a shelter nearby and waits, his weapons left up in the tree house. When he sees the birds have become used to the house, he steals up the tree before dawn with the aid of a lighted torch. The birds come to dance. He aims his arrow through the palm-wood funnel and lets it fly. A bird falls and is picked up by his companion below. The other birds think it has just flown off and they carry on, so he picks off some more before they depart in alarm. Then he skins the carcasses and sews them together into the proper shape for dance decorations.

Another way to catch these plumaged birds is to make a blind beside a pool where they drink. You can easily see the places they have scratched with their feet as they drink; the marks are on all the little branches and bushes around. The hunter sets up his palm-wood pipe again, wedging it firm with moss against wooden supports. The birds come down and think, "That will be a nice place to dive into and refresh myself." As they perch on the branches, they are shot.

Now as to marsupials, these cannot be caught by day; we must wait until there is a good moon, and we go out to examine the trees whose fruits and nuts they eat.[7] We hear them rustling above us as they gnaw and nibble at the nuts and leaves,

---

[6] (On stamps, for example; a bird like it is also on Papua New Guinea's flag.)
[7] The *wotil, menaplka, poembukla, elua, wantep;* they also eat casuarina needles and cordyline leaves.

then we silently hide in a thicket and spy on them. When we see one we shoot it; it tumbles down and we strike it on the head.[8]

Another thing in the Jimi is the large lizard *nggona*. It has a sharp pointed head like a stake and a big body behind. It is just like a crocodile, with big legs and arms and a fat stomach. When its skin is itchy, it makes mudbaths for itself, and there we come upon it and spear it.

There are so many different kinds of game in the Jimi. When we men of the mountain areas to its south grow tired of our own places, we always like to visit there and suggest to our friends and relatives that they organize a hunt for some kind of wild foods or special delicacy which they have.

One of these delicacies is the *uya* nut. When it ripens, the men take their families out into the big bush to collect and cook it; one man will try to take perhaps four women and four youths to help him. The women take out huge netbags of taro, yams, and bananas. They all sleep in big communal shelters or else settle themselves in caves that are warm and dry. A single *uya* tree bears thousands of nuts, which fall to the ground encased in large shells, containing from four to eight individual nuts. Wild pigs get at the nuts by treading on these shells and cracking them. They lie like so much gravel on the forest floor. The men also climb the trees to get them, making ladders and carrying long crooks with which to hook the nuts and make them come crashing down with a thud on the forest floor beneath so that people far away can hear.

The women are told to come and they make successive journeys, carrying the nuts back to the camp in their netbags. Then they begin the long business of preparing the nuts to make them edible. The men break down branches of big trees and make a huge pyre on which to heat the cooking stones for the ovens. To protect themselves against the intense heat when they pick out the stones, they must use extra-long tongs and wear bunches of cordyline leaves hung about their bodies. The oven trenches they make are long and deep too, and teams of men work at each one. They line them with greens and then tip all the netbags full of nuts right in, like so many stones into big pools. They add water, place the cooking stones, and cover the whole thing over with earth.

When they remove the nuts, the first task is to shell them. The men take strong stones and crack the shells open, then pass them on to their wives. It takes a long time, perhaps days, and the work is again done in teams. The wives select out some of the nuts and string them in rows together to be taken home as a special condiment,[9] and the rest they pile up again for the next stage of work.

While the ovens are steaming, the men scatter to the bush, to hunt a little, to wash, and to cut numbers of leaves of a banana-like plant which they then bring back in bundles. The women meanwhile make baskets[10] for trapping birds and carrying food. The men now lay out a single huge netbag stiffened at the bottom with canes. They line this with many different layers of ferns, greens, and tree

---

[8] *Mokelip, öit, kokla,* and *rakop* are among those caught.

[9] *Uya mbar.* (The *uya* is *Pangium edule,* also found elsewhere in the Highlands, for example among the Anga and the Duna peoples.)

[10] *Pimb wal.*

leaves,[11] packed in tightly and firmly, and the banana-like leaves also. Into this they eventually tip all the cooked and shelled nuts, gathering up the sides of the netbag with care. They lace it all over with pliant canes, making these into a net-bag pattern, and bring all the strands to a single point at the top, which they fasten to a stout stake from which it will be suspended. All this work is done close to a suitable pool of water. When the canes have been bound around tightly and firmly, they drag the whole assemblage over to the water and lower it to the bottom of the pool, suspending it by the stake from two crooks of nearby trees. At its top they construct a shelter of leaves and wood against the rain, which might cause the netbag to rot. Then they go home. At this time they eat only the nuts they have reserved as a condiment. They heat these on stones and dry them further in the sun till they are quite hard and keep well. They use them for chewing and spitting out along with salt and ginger on mixtures of blood, fat, and greens that we make when we cook pork.

Two months or three months may go by. Then they call on all their friends and relatives from far and near to bring piles of fresh greens and come to the pool where the nuts have been in storage. With care they lift out the big bundle and lay it down. It is left for a day. The day after, they undo it, pulling apart the layers of rotting matted leaves, and there the clusters of nuts stand up stiffly, like lumps of white mud. These they take for recooking. They fill them into lengths of bamboo already cut and drilled for the purpose, along with very large quantities of greens, and they hand each bamboo out to a relative, a sister, a brother, a nephew, a friend, everyone. The people eat plenty of the greens flavored by the oil of the nuts and leave most of the actual nuts for later. They cook and eat this kind of food several times, enjoying it thoroughly before returning home from the bush.

People speak of the pandanus fruit and the *uya* nut together. This fruit grows in great quantities in the Jimi, and its long spiky fruits stick into each other. To harvest them a man pushes sharply upwards with a long stick, causing the fruit to fall, an action known as "taking the heads of the pandanus." They split the fruits with cassowary bone daggers and steam them. Sometimes we eat this fruit by taking the pips into our mouths, swallowing the oily juice, and spitting the rest out; sometimes we squeeze out the juice by itself and pour it over steamed greens.

When the fruit is in season, our people go down to the Jimi in numbers and carry back loads of the fruit from their friends. They make journey after journey until the season is over. Sometimes they bring back just the oil in bamboo tubes[12] and mix this with greens at home. A similar thing can actually be done with the *uya*. When it forms a mush in recooking, it can be poured into bamboos and then tipped over greens. We wrap the greens in packs and steam them, so they can be cut into portions for visitors and everyone else to share. The packs can be used as formal presentations in bride-wealth and moka exchanges too, or simply as a mark of friendship. The gift will be reciprocated when the recipient cooks his own nuts. The grease of *uya* nuts is as rich as butter, not something to be eaten by

---

[11] *Kim pomba, kim et, wotil omong. Menaplka, minggeklep,* and *upi* leaves are also used.
[12] (See the story at the end of chapter 5. The pandanus fruits ripen in the Jimi before Christmastime, somewhat in advance of those grown at higher altitudes.)

itself. Some people can eat the mush by itself, in spoonfuls, but most prefer to re-cook it and mix it with greens, when it has less of a smell. It keeps well in a con-tainer and can be used for a number of different occasions. The nuts ripen at a time when we are weeding gardens, and by the time we have finished eating them all it is usually the season for pandanus fruit again.

A single pandanus tree bears from four to sixteen fruits, and men in the Jimi plant whole groves of them so they have plenty to give to us when we go as visi-tors to ask for some. We cook some and eat them down there, and others we re-move the inner pith from and make into bundles for carrying away, which the men place under their arms, while the women fill netbags and carry these suspended on their backs. We march off from their settlements back into the forest at dawn. Up at the top of the hill that leads to our place, our own people come up to meet us and may take their share there and eat it before we go down. Some we take home and share with more relatives. The next day a man may be back in the Jimi in search of more.

We never fought with the Jimi people, for we realized that if we did we would have no way of obtaining all those special foods: the nuts, the pandanus fruit, the cassowaries, the wild pig, the fish, greens, all kinds of bird plumage. When our palate tells us it would like to eat something good, that is the only place we can go to satisfy it, so we want to stay good friends with the people there. Some of our girls prefer to be married down there because of these delicacies, and we are happy to send them there. The only disadvantage is that the place is very hot and sweaty, and there is sickness there too. It is difficult to stay inside the houses, so people cook and sleep outside at night, getting bitten by mosquitoes; they don't make fires inside the houses at all, for if they do it is far too hot. After we have visited the Jimi people many times, they grumble and say they want to come and see us. So we convert our sweet potato gardens into stands of wing-beans.[13] We grow large crops of these for their tubers, along with a number of special ba-nanas. When we dig up the tubers, we call on our friends from the Jimi and steam-cook these for them. We say to them, "In your place you have many good foods, we have only the wing bean tuber, so we give you this now." In our area there are many people but not many different kinds of food, whereas in the Jimi it is the other way round: there are only a few people, but there is a huge area of bush filled with all kinds of food.

It was on one of my visits to the Jimi, in 1965, that I learned of the death of my eldest son, Kuma, back at home. He had decided to go to the Hagen show,[14] many miles away from home. We told him he should not, for there were enemy tribes on the way who would kill him if he went by himself, but he would not lis-ten. On the way he stayed with his mother's sister's husband, Mae, a Kope tribesman who lives with the Minembi. When he left Mae's place the next day and came to the Gumants River, he fell in and was drowned. Did our enemies push him in? Or did he simply slip as he was washing himself? Who knows?

---

[13] (*Psophocarpus tetragonolobus,* a nutritious plant regarded as a delicacy. Its leaves, flowers, bean pods, and tubers are all edible.)

[14] (A biennial show organized originally as an agricultural show, with displays of dancing by people from different areas which attract tourists from other countries.)

I was far away in the deep bush of the Jimi cooking *uya* nuts. We were just about to lift the nuts out of the oven when the news came to me. From earlier cookings they had given me many presents of cooked nuts and fish, and we had these slung on poles and were carrying them through the forest to lay them down near a shelter when the man who came as messenger, Ruri of our Kurupmbo clan-section, met us. He said, "Oh, while you've been away something bad has happened at home." "Oh, what is it?" "Your son who went to the show, he has come home very sick, we're looking after him." My heart caved in and felt spongy, and I understood what he meant. I told the people to go and put back into the river the traps full of fresh fish they had given me, and I would collect them later. I set off for home, letting the others come later with the nuts.

We slept overnight in the open forest and the next day we came up to Mbukl and found him lying out in a men's house there. "What happened?" I said. "We don't know. He fell in the river." We put him in a coffin and took him out to the Mount Hagen hospital where they placed him in the ice-chamber. The doctor cut him open and examined him to see if anyone had hit him. "No," they said, "he has just drowned; otherwise there is no mark on him." Nothing to be done then. We took him home and buried him. I wanted to take someone to court for killing him but how could I? So many people had gone to the show, and he had been traveling by himself. Later I cooked twenty pigs for his funeral feast, I invited everyone to come and divided the pork out to them all.[15]

---

[15] (This was in November 1965. After the shock of the death, Ongka threw himself into raising pigs for this occasion and organizing it.)

13 / Moka

Now let me talk again about how I make moka.[1] On ceremonial ground after ceremonial ground I have done this. I have given war-compensation payments[2] to many different clans, starting a long time ago, in the days when we did it all with pearl shells, laying them out on rows of fern and banana leaves. I have given them *kng enda* too. This is when we give a number of pigs without calling out the names of individual exchange partners and without receiving big solicitory gifts[3] in advance. We give it to all the men of a group together as a payment for a killing we have inflicted on them or they have incurred in fighting for us as allies. I have added extra numbers of pigs over and above the ones solicited for in many cases. These extra ones are called *nde olkal kng* because we tie the pigs up to a single ceremonial stake made of *olka* wood and make our speeches next to them.[4] On these occasions I wore special decorations: the big plaque of multicolored feathers set on a backing,[5] and the pale-blue crest feathers of the King of Saxony bird.[6] I made these moka gifts along with the men of my own clan, the Mandembo, at different times and in different years. Sometimes we did the dance in which we bend our knees and make our long aprons sway out in front of us;[7] sometimes we did the stamping dance in which we move round the ceremonial ground in a procession.[8] We did all this many times, until it was all completed, and I was tired of it. On ceremonial ground after ceremonial ground I had done this again and again, and on these same sites the cordylines planted at their edges grew old and gray, the special round houses at the head of the grounds tumbled down, and weeds grew up.

I myself became a boss boy, a tultul, a luluai, and then a local government councilor. It was close to the time of self-government,[9] and Parua[10] had become,

---

[1] (For an account of the technicalities of this kind of exchange, see A. J. Strathern, *The Rope of Moka,* Cambridge, 1971.)

[2] Called *wuö peng,* "man-head" payments.

[3] (These are given to encourage partners to make the main gifts later.)

[4] I gave *wuö peng* to two clans of Minembi, the Kimbo and Yelipi, and these payments included both pigs and shells. I gave in shells to the Tipuka Kengeke clan. I gave *wuö peng,* both pigs and shells, to our own Kundmbo clan, and the same to our Membo clan, with *nde olkal* pigs as well. I gave the same to the Tipuka Oklembo, with whom we had fought so bitterly. I gave all these kinds of gifts too to the Tipuka Kendike clan. These are some of the moka gifts I have made.

[5] *Köi wal.*

[6] *Köi ketepa.*

[7] The *mörl* dance.

[8] The *nde mbo kenan* dance.

[9] (In Papua New Guinea the year of self-government was 1973; independence followed in 1975.)

[10] (Otherwise spelled "Pörwa" or "Peruwa.")

since 1972, our member for the national House of Assembly.[11] The times had changed, and I thought to myself that I would take off my bark belt, my cordyline sprig rear-covering, and my apron, and I would follow the new ways.

It seemed to me that we no longer had men of the old style who could do the hard work of rearing pigs or the women to make the strong netbags for harvesting the sweet potatoes, or to make the pig-ropes and fasten them on the pigs, and so, if I waited much longer, we would not be able to make another moka in the good old way. We used to speak of those women of the old times as wearing long straw-colored aprons with short pig-ropes tucked into them. Over their hair, which they wore in ringlets, they placed a piece of barkcloth, and on top of this they carried their large working netbags. These were the kind of women who could do the work to raise pigs, and now there were none like that left. Such women could raise many, many pigs, both sows and barrows. The pig herd would cluster at her housedoor in the early morning, squealing for their feed of sweet potatoes. There were enough pigs to use for many different things. With one, for example, I could make an initiatory gift in moka;[12] another I could give away in cooked form and get some smaller ones back; with another I could contribute to the ritual performed when we lit a fire in a new men's house or sacrificed at the center post in such a house. With yet another I could contribute to the cooking with which we end a period of mourning after a death.[13] And so on. I am really talking about whole sets of pigs here, not just single ones. If women did not work hard and raise pigs for us, how could we do all this? We depend on them for their work.

I used to tell my womenfolk not to run around showing themselves off, not to wear strings of beads or flashy pieces of printed cloth, and not to tip talcum powder over themselves. They listened to me and they reared many, many pigs, and these I gave away or cooked and distributed on all those ceremonial grounds, until now the cordylines have bowed their heads in an arch toward the earth. On their gray branches the jawbones of the pigs I have cooked are lined up,[14] and the bones themselves have grown green with age. Now, since the white men came, I have watched to see if women of this strong type are still with us, but what I see now is something different. In the morning we used to think first of feeding the pigs or cutting wood, but what the modern girl does is this: she runs to a little pool, with a towel round her neck, soap in hand, to wash and make herself pretty. She smears her knees and her head with scented oil, she arranges her beads and sprinkles powder over them, and then off she goes to smile and make eyes at some smart little fellow wearing a pair of long trousers.

I saw this kind of business and thought, "The old ways have had it now. Everyone's gone crazy." I was the local government councilor for the whole Kawelka tribe at this time, and I decided, "Well, if the old ways must go, let's at any rate do

---

[11] Now the PNG Parliament.

[12] (A present given to encourage a partner to give a bigger moka gift in return later.)

[13] (In this ritual, the relatives of a dead person cook pork and distribute it to all who helped at various stages of mourning for the dead, by helping to bury the corpse, by crying for it, and by bringing in gifts of food and firewood.)

[14] (It is customary to hang up pigs' jawbones in this way in commemoration of their being cooked for particular occasions.)

something as our last big show." So I called on all the men from each small group inside our three clans[15] to come to my place at Mbukl, and I said to them, "Our fathers were true big-men, but their sons are wearing long trousers and drinking beer and are really rubbish-men now. Our mothers were strong women, but their daughters have gone light-headed. The edges of the big gardens we used to make are covered with weeds. Self-government and independence are here, and the old ways will disappear, but let us do one thing before that happens, so that all the groups around and all the white men too will say, "The Kawelka put on a little show, we saw it." Now the old ways will be shaken off as we shake clods of earth from a stump of a tree, and we will take on the new ways. Everything's crazy now, so let us just do this one thing before it all happens. Listen to what I say and go."

I had shot a cassowary bird up in the forested headwaters of the Möka River, and this I cooked for them to eat while we talked. I told them further, "Go to all your relatives and friends and ask for gifts. Make the initiatory gifts to them and prepare to pull in the returns to make a big moka. We will give all the things which are customary: cassowaries, decorating oil, all kinds of valuable shells, cattle and special farm-raised pigs (which have become available since the white men came). We will also give some things that others have never given before, to make our name. In the old days, when our fathers gave moka, they made their name by giving large cassowaries from the place Kora in the Jimi Valley where stone blades[16] were manufactured in the past or by giving *kum kokop,* special little pearl shells with magical power which they hung from the back of their heads. We Kawelka made our name in the past too by giving away a woman in moka as a wife for the Kitepi clan leader, Kuri, father of Parua. People spoke of our doing this and asked others, "Have you done that?" Now, so that our sons in turn may be able to say that their fathers did something notable, let us give now what others have not given." I spoke like this to them without revealing exactly what I meant.

Parua was elected as our member of the national House of Assembly. However, because of a car accident and the death of a driver from the Nengka tribe, Parua was attacked by the man Nengka Ruing.[17] That man was a man of little status and no sense, he was a fool. We all wanted to kill him in revenge, but how could we? He was safe in jail. As a result of this attack Parua was very sick in Port Moresby[18] hospital for a long time. When he returned to our area, he said to us, "You cried for me when I was wounded, you put mud on your skins in mourning for me, you tried to kill my enemies for me, it was your car which carried the men

---

[15] (Mandembo, Membo, and Kundmbo.)

[16] *Tinggrina* blades.

[17] (In 1967 a Nengka tribesman driving a truck through Parua's area knocked down and injured an old man. In revenge the kinsmen of the man set on the driver and battered him to death. Parua was away from the area and had nothing to do with the event; moreover, a large compensation payment was rapidly raised within Dei Council (Parua's electorate) and paid to the Nengka people. Nevertheless, Parua was subsequently attacked and seriously injured by a Nengka man, Ruing, who declared that he had not received proper compensation for the death. Ruing was sentenced to ten years in jail after trial in the Papua New Guinea Supreme Court. Bad feeling between the Nengka's council area (Mul) and Parua's (Dei) continued for many years. See chapter 15 for a song composed by Ongka on this incident.)

[18] (Papua New Guinea's capital city.)

who struck at the Nengka man Kerua in revenge for my wound, although they did not quite kill him.[19] Now I want to give you something, while I am still young and alive. When I die my clansmen may choose to make death-compensation payments to another group, so I want to give you something now.[20]" Parua, of course, is the son of our Membo clanswoman Nomane, whom we gave in marriage to Kuri as part of a moka gift so many years ago.

With these words Parua gave us four sets of eight pigs, to be distributed among all the Kawelka, because we had cried for him and had felt pain on his behalf when he was wounded. He added a cassowary, which we cooked and ate. So I called all our people together and said to them, "See, these gifts have come to us. We do not have women now who will raise pigs for us the way women used to do. Our women used to rear pigs for us men, I built men's houses, I paid death compensations, I gave away pigs in moka. But now what do they do? The modern girl goes off to the stream with her towel, soap, and comb. She washes herself and powders her neck, and then she goes out to smile at men and look for money. Those women of the old times, they put on girdles at their waist, covered their hair with a head-net, carried sweet potatoes in huge netbags. Today's girl walks out and about and lets the weeds grow over the sweet potato garden. She won't rear pigs any more. Self-government is close at hand, and the whole place is turning silly. I am calling this meeting for all of you men of our different clans; each man should go back home and think about it. Go back to your places and rear pigs, talk to your exchange partners from other clans, and prepare yourselves. Let your women put on the old-fashioned working clothes and tend their pigs. I am a man who built men's houses and lit the ritual fire in them, who laid out new ceremonial grounds, who paid compensation for killings, who cooked pigs, who gave live pigs away. Now I have paid for the government tractor to come and expand our ceremonial ground and straighten it out, to pull out tree stumps and level its surface. I paid ten dollars a day for the tractor until fifty dollars were spent. Before that, I took on our own men as workers on the same job and paid them; some received two dollars, some five dollars each. When they were tired of the work, I hired the tractor. Remember this was not done to make a private garden for me, it was for our moka.

Look what is happening to our men nowadays too. It is not only our women who are going crazy. In the old days a man grasped his spade and dug the ground, he cut down the tall stands of wild cane-grass, he turned the soil and made tall bananas and sugarcane grow from it, tending and binding them till they came to maturity. Then he had food for his family and enough for his wife to cook for visitors as well, but men don't do that kind of thing now. Our young men wear long trousers and sunglasses, drink beer. Off they go to market with

---

[19] (On the evening after the attack on Parua, a car traveled eastward to a plantation in Dei Council carrying some men who launched an attack on a Nengka tribesman, of a different clan from Ruing. He was not quite killed, and they subsequently offered him compensation.)

[20] (Death-compensation payments, *kik kapa,* are ordinarily made to a person's mother's kin, and Parua is a sister's son of the Kawelka; but he wanted to give them something himself first, while he was still alive.)

betel nut in one hand and pepper leaf in the other, weaving about in the crowd, chewing and spitting.[21] They go to market, to town, to white men's places as laborers, and there they become headstrong and feckless. In the old days young men would shoulder netbags of sweet potatoes to help the women, but now they walk around idle, fancy-free and easy. In the old days they would do the work to make ceremonial grounds and to dig out the pits for earth ovens, but now they refuse to do all that. The girls put on beads and powder, make eyes, flit from one husband to another. They provoke fights, heads are broken open, men are jailed. It's all ridiculous.

Now self-government is close. Let us just do this one thing before it all goes quite crazy. Before, when we Kawelka gave moka to the Tipuka, we did something which made our name for us. The usual gifts are pigs, cassowaries, shells, pork, decorating oil; but no one had ever given what we gave, a woman, the Kawelka woman Nomane, at the Mbukl ceremonial ground. We gave her as a wife for the leader Kuri, and so we "won" and increased our prestige. She became the mother of Parua, and now in turn he has brought four sets of pigs and a cassowary to us. What shall we do? Each one of our clans has its place in the moka. We plant our stakes to which the pigs are tied in separate rows on the ceremonial ground. We plant these again and again until they reach well out beyond the ceremonial ground. But these are for the gifts which everyone knows. What new thing can we give now? Let us give a car."

"How can we afford it?" they said. The price then was $3,600 including the money for licensing and insuring it. We collected the money and also paid the plane fare down to Lae on the coast for someone to go and fetch it, bringing it back by the Highlands Highway. When he returned with it everyone exclaimed, and some famous big-men[22] came down to our place to see if it was true. I directed them all to check with Parua and see for themselves. At our big moka we gave away as many as twenty cattle as extra gifts. We purchased twenty commercially raised pigs and added these to our own home-reared ones. We gave forty cassowaries. As for our own pigs, how could you possibly count them?

At the head of the row of pigs I put my own pigs: Rut Pepa, named after our place Rut, or Mbukl. It is the one I wagered against the money cultists, and I had Andrew take a picture of it which I still keep. Next in the line was my Rut Wane, then Poklök Wane, then my Rut Pokl.[23] These were the four pigs with personal names which I gave. As extra gifts I myself bought two cows and gave them away. The car[24] too was purchased as a result of my persuasion; we all contributed to its price. They spoke of me and said, "He should have stayed at home and made his own gardens so as to eat food, but instead of that it's as if he's burning up his

---

[21] (Betel nut is a mild narcotic, chewed by highlanders nowadays in imitation of a long-established coastal practice. The red juice from the nut is either swallowed or spat out.)

[22] Men such as Rumba of the Ukini tribe, Mel of Kumndi tribe, Wamb-Wan of Mokei.

[23] (Poklök is the name of Ongka's other settlement place, besides Mbukl. Wane means "one," that is, "a big one." Pokl means "fat," "ripe," or "mature.")

[24] (A gray Toyota Land Cruiser, which Parua began to use long before the final moka ceremony.)

A Tipuka man of the Kitepi Kolkal sub-clan surveys the pigs at a moka. His head-dress includes a pair of hawk's wings (1970s).

Ongka with his pig Rut Pepa, given away in the 1974 moka.

money in a fire. What is he doing?" It was all done as my last big show. This is what I said to them in my ceremonial speech:

> Whoever you are,
> From whatever clan or tribe,[25]
> All you men of different ancestors,
> Hear me.
> Before the white man came,
> When we were by ourselves,
> I dug the ground with a piece of wood,
> I cut the grass with a wooden knife,
> I shaped a stone and called it an ax,
> I raised pigs, I cooked them,
> I made moka,
> I paid for deaths.
> Now the government will go,
> And we shall be by ourselves again
> With self-government.

[25] (Ongka names them: Kengeke, Kendike, Akelke, Oklembo, Ndikambo, Wanyembo (all clans of Tipuka tribe); Maplke and Palke, Epi Kurup, Rulke and Romalke; Kumngaka and Kendipi, Roklaka and Waklpke, Nggolke and Nölka, Kumndi and Römndi.)

The M.P. Parua-Kuri in modern dress poses with Ongka at the Maninge dance in 1971. Parua wears a Lions club cap, Ongka his 'mayoral' chain.

Ongka dances in 1971 beside a clansman, Raema, who became his rival in 1974.

Ongka discusses pigs with two old leaders of Membo clan, at an internal moka between Membo sub-clans.

Ongka at a meeting with his father-in-law Ndamba (the father of Rumbukl) and others of Ndamba's sub-clan. Ongka visited Ndamba to ask for more pigs.

But now
Where are the women's working clothes, their head-nets,
Where are their digging sticks, their girdles,
Where are their heavy netbags for carrying food?
As for the men,
Where are the big gardens they used to make?
Where are their working tools?
They make small gardens now instead of big.
Where have they run away to?
Instead of pigs in our pastures
Now we see chickens surrounded by fences.
There are trade stores and bulk stores,
Plenty of foreign food in them.
The men to cook pigs for sacrifices are gone,
The men to give pigs away in moka are gone,
They are not here.
Now, as to our women,
This is the last dance.
I finish all our old ways.

1971. *Ongka poses with his married daughter Ndau and his young daughter Yara, ready for the dance at Maninge.*

With feathers of the eagle,[26]
With decorated girdles,
With bright cordyline leaves,
With oil rubbed on the skin.
Now the old netbag is thrown into the fire,
Tipped into a hole in the ground,
The netbag of the mothers.
Instead the daughters take up
A bright red netbag,[27]
Wrap cloth around their bodies,
Hang a towel on their head,
And off they go to town,
To squabble over betel nut
And share it with men in the street.
The men play cards,
The women do too.
This whole place has gone crazy.

All my strong things from the past,
Here at Mbukl, my home,
I bury them in my ground.
The things of the women, of their mothers and grandmothers,
The things of the men, of their fathers and grandfathers,
I finish them all.
I finish them with a car,
I finish them with cattle,
I finish them with purchased pigs,
I finish them with cassowaries,
I finish them with our own pigs,
I finish them with tubes of decorating oil,
I finish them with a motor bike,
Now I have finished this matter.
Women who used to wear string aprons
Have broken our custom by wearing cloth.
Men have broken it by wearing trousers.
With their cloth and their combed hair they have broken it.
Where are all the head-nets,
The decorated bark belts,
The woven armbands,
The nosepieces of conus shell,
The aprons inset with marsupial fur?
They have all gone away somewhere.
The ceremonial axes of stone, the carved spears,
The women's head-nets, their capacious netbags,
The pig ropes, the wooden spades,
Where are they all?

[26] (He is referring to the women's decorations worn at the moka dance.)
[27] (Made from imported dyed cloth or wool.)

These things they used
To rear big pigs,
To bring them out for display,
To make gifts to other groups,
All these old things of ours have gone away.
Now these gifts I make to you,
Wrapped as for a funeral.
Take them to the House of Assembly
Where you are a member.[28]

If you are strong,
Later you will make returns to me,
And I shall eat the returns and become old,
The young men will eat them too
And become strong men.
But if you are not strong,
It will be like the time when
The man[29] was lying sick
And said to the ritual expert,
I see those bright red nuts[30] in your bag.
If you cure me, it will be by their power,
If you kill me, it will be by their power."
So, Parua, if you really have the power,
You will make returns to me.
You are going to the House of Assembly,
You talk of self-government,
You talk of independence,[31]
You say, "Soon I will do it."
Have you the strength?
If you bring back strength with you
From the House of Assembly,
Show it to me, let me see it.
Cassowaries I give into your hand,
Pigs I give into your hand,
A car I give into your hand,
A motor bike, cattle, all these I give.
In other places, if they make moka,
They give pigs but not cassowaries,
Or if they give both these things,
They do not give cows as well.
If they give cows,
They do not purchase special pigs as well.
If they give purchased pigs,
They do not give a motorbike,

[28] (The chief recipient of the gift, Parua, was at that time a member of Parliament for Dei electorate in PNG.)

[29] Mambokla Öpni.

[30] *Kela kur mong.*

[31] (Independence was actually achieved in September 1975, about a year after Ongka made this speech.)

Or if they give a bike,
They do not give a car.
But now I have put all these things together
Into your hand.
Now it is your affair.
The car is for you only,
But the money, how many hundreds of pounds,
Lying straight, lying sideways,[32]
There is a hundred for each of the little groups
Inside your two clans.[33]
Take it all.
Whatever you do with it is your affair.
You may give it to Akelke,
You may give it to Kendike,[34]
That is up to you,
I don't know.
You are a man who goes after girls,
You play cards, you drink beer.
If you do that, it is up to you.
For my part I leave my strong things in your hands now.
You members talk of self-government,
You talk of the House of Assembly.
Will your work go straight
Or will it go crooked?
I do not know.
Before, when Australia was here,
I worked alongside the white men,
They helped me and I helped myself.
Now it is up to you members.
What you will do I do not know.
Eat my gifts and go.

There was a lot of work in getting together all those presents for the actual handover. It took us a day to drag all the pigs up to the ceremonial ground, another to bring in the cassowaries, another to muster the cattle; we counted them all off on a piece of paper. There were so many we had to make a big fence and put the cattle inside to stop them straying. "This is my show, I am making it here at my place, Mbukl, on my own ground," I said. "If anyone is willing to come forward and take the knotted cordyline from me, let him do so. See how many things we have given, pigs which are our own and ones we have bought with money, cassowaries, decorating oil, cattle, a motorbike, a car, and money as well. If anyone thinks he can match all of these things, let him take the knotted cordyline leaf from me as a sign now."[35] No one took up the challenge. So I finished my show after very many years of planning, after holding several small moka in preparation, after saying so

[32] (The money is laid out ceremonially on the dancing ground prior to being handed over.)
[33] (The Kitepi and Oklembo clans.)
[34] (Other Tipuka clans.)
[35] (As a sign that his group would be the next to make a moka and it would be comparable to Ongka's.)

1980s. A subsequent moka, at the place Kuk. Ongka counts pigs on his fingers, reckons the number needed.

Ongka, Ruk, Koepa, and Yap, all of Ongka's sub-clan, consider a stake to which a pig will be tethered for a moka.

Ongka surveys the pigs.

Ongka makes a speech. Note the lack of decorative attire on this occasion.

many times that I would do it. In the end I did bring it off. I wrapped all the strong things of men and women from the past and laid them in their grave with my last big moka.

It was not long after this that Opa, the brother of my cousin, Ken, died. Ken is an important man and I was upset. So we got busy again and raised things for the funeral feast, we bought sixteen cattle and took several of our own pigs and cooked all of these together for the visitors. I spoke: "Did you people not get those white men's tools, the ax, the spade, and the bushknife, as I did? We use those tools to clear away undergrowth and turn the soil and grow sweet potatoes. Our wives feed these to the pigs and they grow fat, so we can use them. Did you not hear about how to do all that? I suppose you don't have any of these things like pigs, so you have come once more to eat mine here." Hundreds of people came and they all received pork from me and went.

A big-man[36] came and said "We thought we'd catch up with you, and do as you do. You bought cars, and then so did we. But you won over us by obtaining a gun.[37] So we thought we'd try to get guns too, but then you made your big moka and pushed ahead of us again. We thought you might be equaled in that, but then you went and purchased a new car. After that we thought perhaps we too would get more cars, but now you have put more pigs together and cooked them here. It is clear we have no chance of catching up with you. You are a strong man and you have your own power!" I replied, "My show is over now. If you want to make moka again, don't plan it on a big scale. I can't see the sort of people around now who will make big returns to you. Let's do something else now. At any rate, mine is over, I have buried it at Mbukl. The women with hands to rear pigs have gone, the men with hands to make gardens have gone, if we try it again it won't work." So if Parua does make returns to us, item for item, that will be good, but it will take drive on his part. It was I who drove the Kawelka people on at each step to come out and do it, so that our reputation would be made. If Parua can do that, well and good. After all, he's an MP and he goes to the Parliament; if he is a truly strong man he will make returns to us. If he doesn't, well, in the old days we Kawelka gave his mother in moka to the Kitepi clan, that was how he was born. If he doesn't make returns to us, I have finished the business with cassowaries and pigs and made my speech; I couldn't turn back on all that and make some kind of court case out of it if he fails to pay us back. That is not done. I would say to him, "All right, my sister's son." Now the story of how I made my moka is over.

---

[36] Tipuka Kelmbo Ongka.

[37] (Gun licenses are hard to obtain in the Highlands because of a ban on killing birds of paradise with guns and also because of problems related to tribal fighting.)

14 / White Men Come and Go

I will tell you again about the white men and how they came to our place.

The first things we saw were the airplanes. We thought they were hawks or that their sound came from rats running through the grass, but later we learnt that these planes brought "the people with wealth." Previously when we married or made moka we did not have many things; we just had a few small nassa shells and cowries and pieces of green snail shell. The man who had these things was a big-man to us at this time. "Why was it he who found those things?" we would say in envy. Then the white men, the Kewa Klalke, the men with wealth, came to us. At first they did not come right down to us in what is now Dei Council. They came to stay in Kelua near to Ogelbeng, some 20 miles away from us to the south. There was warfare on at the time. How could we go there directly to see them?

Later a white man came to a place quite nearby,[1] and we heard that he was giving out nassa shells in return for food and work. We set straight out for his place with our tools and he asked us to cut down the bush and clear the area of cane-grass. We worked at this in stretches of a week or two weeks, and he would give each one of us a pile of shells after that. "The owner of shells has come," we said, and we gladly did his work for him. When we had the shells, we spent hours filing off their backs, piercing them, and sewing them together to form shell mats backed with moth cocoons.[2] We made bigger and bigger mats and we said, "Now we'll be able to obtain a wife with these." It was Mr. Bob Gibbes[3] who came, and later Mr. Ross came too. They made an airstrip and brought in coffee seeds by plane. We watched them making holes in the ground and wondered if they were planting nut or fruit trees. Later we saw the coffee trees growing and learned that when it was harvested and cooked it had a nice smell. He brought in pearl shells, bushknives, spades; all these things he gave to his workers. He did not give them money. We didn't like money at that time; we thought it was something strange and we wanted to have all the strong things we really knew about already. Mr. Bob brought in all these things for his plantation by his own airplane.

Later Mr. John Collins[4] came. He brought in a secondhand jeep and struggled through with it on the first road down to the place Tiki. He was a very determined

[1] Pingapöngamb (also called Penga, subsequently the site of the Dei Council chambers).

[2] The cocoon is a strongly spun outer shell, which contains large numbers of young and is big enough to use as a backing in this way.

[3] (An entrepreneur and pilot who earlier had run Gibbes-Sepik Airways. The plantation he made in the early 1950s is known as Tremearne, at Penga, in Dei Council. He later built a number of hotels in the Highlands, then retired to Australia.)

[4] (This was in the mid-1950s. John Collins came from a well-known business family in the Highlands and was the nephew of Danny Leahy, one of the early Australian explorers and farmers

and skillful driver and forced his vehicle over steep and muddy hillsides to get into Tiki. There he planted coffee in the flat valley area, inhabited by poisonous snakes and wild spirits, a place which we had left uncultivated before because of its dangers. He set up a huge plantation and brought in workers from Chimbu, Wabag, Tari, Mendi, Pangia, Ialibu,[5] all the distant places. He paid them in cash, and from his coffee he himself drew in large amounts of money. He built a big factory by himself and processed his coffee on the spot and sent it straight off to the international markets in big 6- or 7-ton lorries. He worked on a big scale. He had so many laborers that on a single pay day he would use up £1,000.

When Mr. Bob came we had accepted nassa shells, made mats with them, and paid bride-wealth and moka gifts with them, but John now told us that money was the really strong thing with which to buy cars and all the white men's property, so we listened and said, "All right." We took money off to the trade stores, and when we showed it there we got knives, axes, clothes, saucepans, everything we wanted. "Ah," we thought. "The things we thought were strong were not really so, they were just rubbish bits of shell thrown up on the coast. Now we see that money is the really strong thing, and we want it." So we have given up all the old valuables, snail shells and the like, and we call money our new highway.

At first we had no white man or other outsider actually staying with us. Then Mr. Black, a government officer, sent the policeman Mberem[6] to stay with me and we made a station at Mbukl. Policeman Jimi, who, like Mberem, was from Madang, was posted to Mala (some 8 miles off to the east), Arit of Morobe was sent to the place Korn (near to Mount Hagen town), and Nalinge was posted to Maplka (over in what is now Mul Council). They were all told that if anyone made trouble they should arrest them and bring them in to the government officer. These officers (kiaps) themselves came to see us from time to time.

At Reipamul Father Ross[7] came to stay. At Kuta Mick and Dan Leahy[8] came and made their sluices and runways in search for gold among the river stones. The earliest government officer, Mr. Murray Edwards, was at the place known as Klomet (later Mount Hagen town). At Ogelbeng were Vicedom and Strauss,[9] who were Lutheran missionaries. They took in people as their workers, taught them how to write, poured water on their heads in baptism, and told them not to fight or steal. They told us that they were working for the dead and for the living, and that one day the dead would come alive again. They built churches and sang

in the Hagen area. John Collins's highly productive plantation in Dei Council was taken over in 1975 by the council itself, some time after his death. It has since fallen into disuse, and individual sections of it have been taken over by local growers.)

[5] (All places in other Highlands provinces of PNG.)

[6] (See the accounts in chapters 4 and 10.)

[7] (A Catholic priest who became famous in the area. He died in 1974 and was given a ceremonial funeral by the Mokei tribesmen with whom he had lived and worked.)

[8] (Two of the initial explorers of the Highlands, who settled in PNG. See M.J. Leahy and M. Crain, *The Land That Time Forgot,* London, 1937.)

[9] (Both wrote fundamental works of scholarship on the Hagen people's culture. See G. Vicedom and H. Tischner, *Die Mbowamb,* Hamburg, 1943, and H. Strauss and H. Tischner, *Die Mi Kultur der Hagenberg Stämme,* Hamburg, 1962.)

songs inside these. Meanwhile all the businessmen came in too and built up their plantations and farms, but no white man came directly to us Kawelka.

Now I'm going to say something further, it's just a foolish word from a silly old man. I'm just going to say it and throw it away. Before the white men came we had no strong tools, we made them from wood and stone only. Our spades were shaped from wood, our axes from river stones. We sharpened the edge of a casuarina branch and made a knife with that, shaping one end into a handle and the other into a blade. The blade was not really sharp, and we prepared numbers of these tools for a single day's work. We used up many of them together, cutting our way gradually through the undergrowth of a garden area. We had our own stone axes, bound with bark at the handle. We had our salt, which we fastened up in round or long packs.[10] We had our decorating oil,[11] which we keep in gourds or in long bamboo tubes. These were the only valuable things we had.

Later, when the white men brought boxes of goods to Mount Hagen, we went to view these, and we saw how strong everything was—hammers, nails, all kinds of tools—so we decided it could not be human beings who made these; it must be the spirits. We thought it must be the spirits of our own dead, who had sent them for us, and the white men were fooling us and taking hold of these things for themselves. We thought that if we had possessed pieces of paper with our mothers' and fathers' names on them we could have shown these and taken the goods for ourselves. But instead the white men were taking them for themselves. Much later in our area people began to say the same thing about money and they started "wind work"[12] to get it, for the white man, they said, had lied about it and money was not really made by them but by our ancestors.

I thought about this problem for some time, but I decided against the other people's ideas. I thought that we here have never in our history before had the same powerful new things as the white people, and so there could be no real strength in what people were saying. Look at the powerful things the white man makes, at how he can travel across water in ships, how he can cross the earth in cars and fly through the air in planes. We could not do that. We used to look at the Jimi River and say, "It's too big to cross. How shall I get over it?" It was a big divide between us and the Jimi people on its northern side. Or we would look at big hawks as they soared and swooped from hilltop to hilltop and say, "Oh, I wish I were a bird and could fly like that!" When the white men brought all their things, I was a young man. My father cried because he was too old to live for long and use them, thinking how in his youth he had worked so hard and long with our own ineffective tools, discarding them rapidly as they grew blunt or broke in pieces. I have never been to the white men's own places—England, America, Australia, China, Japan—but people who have been there say that those are the places where the really strong things are. They say too that these lands are very distant from

---

[10] (Salt was imported into Hagen from the Enga area to the west and the Jimi Valley to the north.)

[11] (This special tree oil, from the *Campnosperma* tree, is traded in from Southern Highlands Province. It is rubbed on the body to make it glisten for ceremonial dances.)

[12] (*Köpkö kongon;* see chapter 11.)

1970s. Ongka at the ceremonial ground Mope, of the Kawelka Membo clan, berates opponents in a dispute. He is acting in his role as a Councillor.

1970s. Ongka and Nikint, a son of Ndamba, wait in an enclosure at Mbukl, to register their votes in a parliamentary election.

ours; they are in darkness when the sun shines on us and we are in darkness when it's daytime with them. For these white people to reach us here in the Highlands it is a long way and it takes them some time to get to us. But they came and brought their things with them.

Now more recently they told us they had been having meetings and had decided on self-government and independence. "What are those things?" we said. We thought there was a danger that our own people would claim too quickly that they had all the knowledge they needed, and that later they would fall down if they rushed it and set up all kinds of people as ministers in a government. There are of course many things which we are ready to do for ourselves. We know how to grow coffee now, how to plant, prune, pick, dry, and bag it for sale, and we shall be able to carry on doing all that. We know about cattle, how to fence them in, give them salt, inject them with medicines, and we can look after them ourselves now. We understand the way local courts work and how to settle disputes; we shall be able to run them ourselves as village courts.[13] We now have our own men who can drive and who can also work as mechanics to fix cars and tractors. But I think there are some things we haven't grasped yet. What about the telephone? When we listen to it, we can get in touch with far-off places like Moresby, Sydney, Canberra, even England. I don't think we understand it yet. Nor do we know everything there is to know about the radio, or about planes. Pilots don't steer planes as men steer cars; they sit and watch their instruments and just touch them and it sails through clouds until it comes out at its destination. Petrol, oil, diesel, all the parts of cars or planes—we didn't invent these things and we don't understand all of them yet.

Some of our people are running too fast and showing off as ministers. If it's just our dead spirits who showed all these things to the white men, well, all right; but if the white men found out these things themselves by their own efforts, then I think we shall soon get into difficulties after our independence. There are some matters which we can handle, but others will get into a mess, and then if we ask people to come back, they may say, "You told us we were finished, and that we should go. What are you calling us back for now?" So if we hurry all these things along and later find we can't manage them, I wonder if we will be a little bit embarrassed or not? The members in the parliament want all the white men to go, but can we manage?

I see quite a lot of plantations,[14] ranches, missionaries' houses, and the like are unoccupied now, and they're falling into disrepair; weeds are springing up and covering them. Do people in the white men's countries know about this? Our ministers and MPs are showing off. We elected them to let white men and ourselves

[13] ('Local courts' are heard by trained magistrates, usually outsiders to the community of those disputing. The Village Courts Act of 1974 provided for the establishment of regular courts run by local people to deal with a range of disputes.)

[14] (The PNG government instituted a program for the repurchase of expatriate plantations by indigenous landowners. The government supplied the money, like as loans or as outright assistance. In the financial year 1975–76 some twenty-two plantations were bought in this way at a cost of K1 million. Subsequently, there have been many problems in the running and financing of these enterprises.

stay together, but they have done the opposite. Of course, this is only nonsense talk from a rubbish-man. Still, when everyone in our area took up the "wind work" money cult and I was the only one to stand out against it, in the end I was proved right and they were all made ashamed. In this matter, I don't truly know about it all. I am just giving my ideas, and I would like them to be known freely by as many people as possible.

15 / Songs

I have finished all the serious talk, and now I'm going to end by telling you about some of the songs I've made up and sung on various occasions.

Some of our songs are courting songs.[1] A number of men join in singing these in the evening while young men actually do the turning-head ceremony with the girls. There was one song I sang in the chorus in this way when the girl Mberem was being courted by Ru.[2] Originally this song was sung for a woman called Kuk of the Minembi tribe, our enemies. Some of us Kawelka had courted her before, but then she married into another clan of her own Minembi tribe.[3] This is the song:

> Rut ya moklp-a kant-mel a
> Kara kin kopa wone ninim a
> Kopa ya ropa peta nöri o
> Le pa pa ya pa wa ya
> Kilt Kuk amb ya kandep oklmba
> Minembi wuö num ile mba ponom-a
> Amb-e wak ri a na rop ond o
> Le pa ya pa pa wa ya.

> Here at Mbukl I see how the mist
> Spreads over the hill at Kin Pup.
> Mist, do not close in like that.
> I've been to Kilt and seen the girl Kuk.
> She's going to the sea of Minembi men,
> But I've not let her go, she's mine.[4]

The next courting song is one which we sang to a girl of the Kendipi tribe. As we were in her house late at night courting her, her mother watched and watched us and stirred up the fire. Her eyes were big and she would not sleep, so we sang this song to say we were going now. In the end this girl and her friend were married to men of tribes near to their own. We were from a more distant group. That time, eight of us young Kawelka men walked out there together, and we took an

---

[1] (Many of these have been translated in A.J. Strathern, *Melpa Amb Kenan*, Port Moresby: Institute of PNG Studies, 1974.)

[2] (An entrepreneur and leader belonging to Ongka's clan and related to him as a "classificatory" wife's sister's husband i.e., Ongka and Ru both married wives of the same clan, Kawelka Kundmbo.)

[3] She was of Mimke clan and she married a Nambakae clansman.

[4] (Published before as song 13 in *Melpa Amb Kenan*.)

older man, Pundukl, to be our companion and to look after the fire. We put a good show on there, ducking our heads down in the ceremony until the ashes from the fire flew up into our faces, but we didn't get the girl because of that watchful mother.

Köi kuri elka maklk elna
Ambokla manem e a ndip kaklnga
Na kond enem a kaemb enem a
Kona röngin kona pöt röngan a
Nanga kopa kong ila mbi ond a
Nanom Ikömb kong ila mbi ond a.

The white bird's plumes sway forward and back.
My girl, your mother stirs up the fire.
It makes me sorry, makes me sad.
Dawn, rise quickly and I'll be off
To my land of mists, to my land of rain.[5]

We were wearing plumes of the white bird of paradise and swishing them forwards and back in the hope that the mother's eyes would become drowsy as she watched, and we could be freer with the girl, but she kept on watching us, so we sang that we would soon be off home to our own misty hills.

The next song is one we sang to a woman called Kae. This was not my own wife Kae, it was another girl of the same name. My own Kae was married to someone else first before she came to me, and I did not actually court her. This song was for the Kae who married Mera in our clan. I helped in the songs for her and I actually did court another girl she brought along with her, but in the end I didn't marry that girl; she went back to her own place. Here is our song to Kae:

Rut ya moklp a kant mel a
Kin kopa ropa wone ninim a
Paruruwaya pa ya epaya pa waya
Mil Kae mep a mbi nilmba
Kae manem kik a rönt ronom a
Paruruwaya pa ya epaya pa waya.

Here at Mbukl I look up and see
Mist clouds over Kin Pup.
I've said that I will take Kae off,
And now her mother gets ready
A bundle of ashes in mourning.[6]

Many of our songs are serious ones, to do with warfare and revenge. We sing them to show our intention to kill or to escape being killed. Here is one:

---

[5] (Published as song 1 in *MAK*. Slight differences appear in this version, as in other cases.)
[6] (Previously translated as song 21 in *MAK*.)

Pint Kanamb o e Kora uimb ninim
o rol nde e
Omba we mba nda
rol ndenge e
We mon e
rol ndenge erol nde

Kanamb, of Pint, he says he'll come
To our place Kora.
If he comes, will he go unharmed?
No, not unharmed.

This man, Kanamb, or Rangk, he was of the Kimbo clan inside the Minembi tribe. Enemies of his in the Andakelkam section of the same tribe wanted to kill him and threatened him in this song. Rangk was a powerful big-man and warrior with piercing eyes like those of an eagle. Looking at him you felt he had eyeballs as tough as those red *kela kur* nuts we find in the forest. He carried a *tinggrina* stone ax with him and put on a headdress of black *mek* feathers. He would walk up softly and look at people sideways with his neck twisted back a bit and say, "There are people like you who go around saying things about our clan." When he spoke like that, people fled in fear. In a single day's fighting he once killed four men and chased away all the neighboring groups! When I was a boy I fought alongside him against the Andakelkam, and I knew how badly they wanted to kill him. Rangk made a reply to their song:

Ei woi pa
Na nu Möka pol a tep a
Angepina pol a tep a
Ei woi pa
Wuö Kora Weipö nt a
Na pi ninim a
Na mbo nil a mbi nda
Ei woi pa a.

I'm bridging the Möka,
I'm bridging the Angepina.
The man Kora Weipö is telling me to go.
If I go then, where does he think I'll go?

This man Weipö was of the Andakelkam group. Rangk was planning to cross the two rivers by making rough bridges of stones and branches, and so to attack Weipö in his own place.

In the end Rangk was not killed in warfare at all. He was poisoned when visiting another place. His enemy Weipö was poisoned in revenge by Rangk's clan. When Rangk died, an Andakelkam leader, Pakl, sang a song to celebrate this. He likened the death of many warriors to the fall of big trees in the forest. Only he himself was left unharmed.[7]

[7] (Pakl finally died of sickness in 1975.)

> Pint kraep wi a runga pelinga
> Mukl Kaepa met a
> Kon Kon o nilinga pint a
> Pint panda wuö ti mor ndi-nt a
> Ok Raem mep a Ui pamb a Nöui pamb a

> The forest beech of Pint falls flat,
> The earth quivers at Kaepa.
> I am a weakling, pushed around
> By all the strong groups, but now,
> Ukini girl Raem, let me take you off
> To Ui and to Nöui.[8]

The "forest beech" was of course Kanamb, or Rangk, himself, and Pakl was telling how pleased he felt at his enemy's death by saying that the earth shook when Rangk fell. Pakl's own group was small and dominated by Rangk's in warfare. Ui and Nöui are the names of two streams at Pakl's place. He was happy at the death of his enemies' leader, and he would celebrate by marrying the girl Raem, who had come to him.

Another time the Kawelka Kundmbo clansmen wanted to kill a Minembi man, Tape, of the Papeke clan. He fled into the hills, and they stood at the edge of their own clan territory, overlooking his place, and sang this song:

> nde rol nde pa win o ye
> Koma Tape—a Mokla Tip ile ponom e
> nde rol nde pa win o ye
> Ekit mek e romba ming ile rop o e
> nde rol nde rol nde pa win o e.

> Tape of Komapana has left his place
> To hide in the hills of Mokla.
> I come to Ekit Kuk
> With big black plumes in a bamboo tube.

Ekit Kuk is the name of the vantage point from which they watched the Minembi hills. The plumes are those of the *mek* bird, which men use to decorate the tops of their shields for fighting. The Kawelka meant that they would still pursue their intended victim and had their war decorations ready, stored in bamboo containers. However, they didn't succeed in catching Tape, and in the end they gave up in fatigue. He is still alive and walking about.

When we hold our dances we make up songs to sing at these too. These are about ourselves, about our groups and other groups around them. Here is one we sang in 1964 when we gave some pigs in moka to two Tipuka clans, the Kitepi and Oklembo, previously our enemies in minor warfare but also our allies in the big fights against the Minembi tribesmen.

---

[8] (*Ui* means "come" and *Nöui* "don't come.")

Kara Rut o
Mukl ko-pil o
Kara Rut o
Wakl ko-pil o
Elkau e o e e e o
Wuö pint o Panda wuö yo
Na Kang o reklaep rop o
Elkau e o e e e o.

On the narrow ridge of Mbukl
We laid our plans
On the narrow ridge of Mbukl.
We hatch them now.
I am a man who was pushed around
By the strong groups here, and so
I can only muster a line of boys
To dance here before you.

The gift of pigs made on that occasion was to encourage the Tipuka to make a much bigger gift to us later, which they did in early 1965. The moka I gave as my last big moka in 1974 was in return for that one we received in 1965.

Sometimes in our moka dances we sing about killing other men too:

Rokl e pint o ngolna pilip o
Kuki ndaep o ndoron eko
Eo e e o elkau
Ipeyo aipeyo e e o
Terema Keap o pöp urum—o
Wöya nim kandep kent olkau
e e e e elkau
Ipeyo aipeyo e e o.

You cut down our tall man,
We tore the bloom from
Your young man's skin.
Kiap from the coast,
It was good you came.
Wöya, I look at you,
And I let you go.

The "tall man" here is Parua, our member of parliament. He was attacked and wounded by a Nengka tribesman in 1970 in revenge for a road accident in 1967 when a Nengka driver died. The driver was a young man and so we sang of our 'removing the bloom' from his fine young skin. Deaths like this would have provoked warfare in the old days, but now the kiap, or government officer, was here we would let the leader of that particular Nengka clan be.

That song was invented by me and sung by our clan at the ceremonial ground called Maninge in 1971 in a preparatory moka occasion leading up to my big one in 1974. Now I want to tell you the one we sang in 1974 itself:

Mul wuö y o e e e o
Mul wuö yo wuö ndimb o ngonom o e e
Elkau e e yo ea ai o pa wa ye
Wuö mon o e e o
Wuö mon o
Kang reklaep o rop o e e
Elkau e e yo ea ai o pa wa ye.

You, you have men,
Their arms linked in long rows together.
But we, we do not have men,
We are few,
A line of boys dancing in a row.

Here we sang of how small we are as a group by comparison with our Tipuka recipients, and so it was a very hard thing for us to complete the moka gift to them. And not all of our men joined in the dance either, because of troubles over a death earlier, so we sang of this too, describing ourselves not as men but as "a row of boys dancing."

We put over another message to the Tipuka on the same occasion:

Rut moklp o kant e na
Ombil köyo namb namb a ninim olkau
e e o e pa wayayo pa Ikau
Wuö ti-o mon nint o
Wuö mon o kang reklaep o rop olkau
e e o e pa wayayo pa Ikau.

Here at Rut I stand and see
Down at the river Ombil
The cordylines wave and want to eat.
I have no men here,
No men here, only boys lined up to dance.

We sang here of the death of our leader Mel, of my own clan, who was poisoned by one of the Tipuka clans in 1962. No compensation was ever made for his death and so we sang of ourselves as "cordylines" wanting to eat. The cordyline is our special sacred shrub, and Mel was buried in a cordyline grove. Next time the Tipuka give to us, they can think of that.

We have many mourning songs, sung when deaths occur in warfare or however. There was the time when Kombukla tribesmen killed ten men altogether of Tipuka Kengeke clan. The widows of two of these men sang:

Niki kundi kan o tilinga o
Pangk mbok wöyö monom o
Na pilip ko e pimb o
Pilip ko e pimb o
Kononga Kowa kin pilip ko pimb o e.

Niki, you killed our men,
And dragged a brown pig around by its rope till it died,
To cook in celebration.

Pangk, the decoration you wore on your nose
Is left without you now.
I will think of him and sleep, of him and sleep,
My man Kowa of the place Kononga.

Later they killed Niki, the Kombukla man, in revenge.

Here is one the mother of a Kawelka man who was killed sang. I have told you about it earlier.[9] The young man was called Ik:

Ik na ko e e
Ik na ka
Kenan Ik ropa
Pela ming o nggau ndonom o

Ik, oh my Ik,
You are dead,
What shall I do?
Ik, the bamboo flute,
On which you played your songs,
Is broken now.

He was a noted flute player, and his mother thought of that as she cried and sang for him. Ik was killed in fighting with the Kombukla too.

Here is another one sung by a mother. Her two handsome young sons were hunted by our Kawelka down among the streams at the border of their territory and ours. We speared them and broke their bones with river rocks. They were of Klamakae tribe.

Tikimb o
Nu Pil ku-nt e
Romba kang mon o e
Tikimb wa
Tikimb e
Tikimb wa
Tikimb e
Nu Angekl ku-nt e
Romba kang o mon o e
Tikimb wa
Tikimb e
Tikimb wa
Tikimb e.

Oh, Tikimb,
The stones of the river Pil,
Tikimb, oh, Tikimb,
The stones of the river Angekl,
They were not for killing you!
Tikimb, oh, Tikimb.

---

[9] (See chapter 6. The other man killed was Kur. The song is the same as given there, although in a slightly different translation.)

We killed Tikimb and his brother Meng first, and later in revenge the Klamakae killed our two clansmen, Oni and Kalimb. The Klamakae used to help the Minembi Andakelkam in warfare against us. They lived down in the valley, and it was hard for us to get at them. They trapped and killed two Tipuka men of Kengeke clan, and we resented this because the Tipuka were our allies. They fastened vines round their necks, choked them, and pushed them into the Angekl River, and then danced in triumph over this. Looking down at them our men were angry. They said, "What kind of a way of killing men is this? Men are not dogs or snakes to be trussed up and choked and thrown into streams." We went and asked for their bodies, offering pork and a cassowary, but the Klamakae came out to fight again and speared one of our men, Krae, in the leg and killed him.

Our men were incensed by this and one day Mökö, of Kundmbo clan, who lived with his mother's people in our clan, led a group out to the hills to intercept a party of Klamakae coming back from the Jimi after arranging a marriage there. Mökö was bold in fighting, like an eagle. The Klamakae were resting at a spot near the point where the Angekl and Pil headwaters meet, eating pork and cooked pandanus fruit, when Mökö crept up on them and with a sudden shout launched his spear. The Klamakae fled down the hill with the Kawelka pursuing, and Tikimb was speared and fell into the river, crushing his bones. Because of this the Klamakae later joined in against us when we had our battle against the Oklembo clan, and finding Oni and Kalimb up in the hills, they killed them and strung them up in vines with their necks broken by ax blows, saying that they had left them like two marsupials for the Kawelka to cook and eat there if they so wished.[10]

Now I come forward to much more recent events. Here in Moresby in 1974 a young man called Wonom of the Tipuka Kitepi clan died,[11] and they said that two of my young men of our Klammbo group, his own cousins, had killed him. The two sent back a sacred divination sign swearing their innocence, but the relatives of Wonom at home would not listen, and they harried me, as the big-man of the group, with threats of killing. In the end I sang this song:

Rut ya moklp a kant mel a
Öurunga kopa ropa wone ninim a
Namb ya nimb a kant mel a
Pukl Kal wuö ya mba Kewa ndom ranom a
Kang pitim noman ea weng nandeklnga
Mökö mam kep ile na mondopa min nonom a
Na pena pep a manga pep a
Keap nitim pukl e a traim etep
Könimb ent a.

[10] (This killing is also mentioned in chapter 6, where the fight with the Oklembo is described.)

[11] (He suffered a coronary attack after a drinking bout. Because he had also been near the scene of some fighting at the time, his clansmen said that Kawelka companions had done this. For a year they threatened Ongka with revenge if compensation was not paid, and in the end Ongka brought this out into the open and reported it to the government. Later, despite the lack of a basis for the accusations against him, Ongka organized a compensation payment to the Kitepi to forestall any further covert taking of revenge.)

I am up at Mbukl and I see
How cloud covers over Urunga.[12]
I would like to speak and reply to their talk,
But our young men are gone and have taken up foreign ways.
The hearts of those men are still not soothed
And down at the banks of the Mökö River
They gnaw at my soul.
What shall I do? Sleeping in the open,
Or in my house, I must try
To see if the kiap's words will help me.

Wonom's clansmen were angry, and they stole all my pigs and big cassowaries, my coffee-pulping machine,[13] everything, and so in the end I took the matter right out in public to the council chambers and revealed everything they had done, including their names. The government officer and other leaders heard this and warned Wonom's relatives not to use those kinds of threats again. The officer fined them twenty kina each and said that if the case came up again it would go to the highest court, the Supreme Court,[14] as a criminal charge against them.

Now, Andrew, what are you going to do with all this talk I have given you? It is up to you, and I want to sing a last song to make that point to you:

Na moklp ond kona mbö
Kona monom o e
Ya Univesiti-nt a salim elinga
Andep mor o e
Wuö ta ye ukl mbö nim tein o e
Ik mbö na nimb a we pamb o e.

The place that I have come from
Is covered by mists and rain.
The university has brought me here,
And I am walking around.
My son, you make all the arrangements now,
I'll just say the words and leave them with you.[15]

---

[12] (An important settlement place of the Kitepi clansmen.)
[13] (Used to remove the red pulp from the coffee bean.)
[14] (Later the PNG National Court.)
[15] (This song was addressed to Andrew, in the hope that he would arrange the publication of what Ongka had spoken.)

Ongka receives baptism into the Catholic Church at the place Raiorong, Kuk, 1989.

Mid-1995. Ongka considers life today in Hagen.

Mid-1995. Ongka considers the future.

Ongka smiles at his house-door, mid-1995.

Ongka drinks a coca-cola.

16 / Yara Speaks

The following is an interview with Ongka's daughter Yara, a young married woman with three children.

Yara is the daughter of Rumbukl, a woman of the Kawelka Kundmbo clan who was herself the daughter of the 'big man' Ndamba. Yara had an elder brother Namba, who died in 1995, and has a younger sister, also married, Tu, by the same mother Rumbukl; also a younger brother David, as yet unmarried. Rumbukl was an energetic and capable woman, whose death from cancer in 1992 was a great loss to her family. Yara, like her siblings, was born at the old settlement Mbukl and grew up there in the 1970s. After her marriage, she visited the new settlement place at Kuk and subsequently after her mother's death built a house there in order to be able to help look after her father and take care of her mother's grave.

Working with Yara as one of our female informants has made us realize how important it is to include the voices of women to help balance and round out the narratives given by men about themselves and their society. Yara was selected especially because she is highly articulate and is one of the children of Ongka with whom we have a continuing working relationship. The interview given here took place in front of Yara's house at Kuk (the small locality name is Poklök), and Ongka himself was present at it and made his replies to his daughter's comments as recorded here. Despite Yara's criticisms of her father's actions she is loyal to him and in 1996–1997 greatly helped him to recover from a stroke. The excerpts included here are from a larger corpus of materials that we have been gathering to document Yara's life story. This interview dates from 1995.

AJS: Please can you say how you feel about not having gone to school.

Yara: He [Ongka] did not put me into school, you know; that was something very wrong that he did. If he had put me into school, I could have found some kind of good job to do. I would have had a nice house to live in, and my hands and face would have looked good. But he did not do this and therefore I had to follow another pathway. You know, I could have disobeyed him and gone against his wishes, but I said, "Well, he is my father," and therefore I stayed at home and I shouldered all the burdens that I had to. And I said, "If I get married I will bring in a bride-price for you." So I worked with my hands, I put a netbag onto my head, I did gardening work, I harvested, I cooked food from the gardens for him. And I said to him, "Why did you force me into doing all these things?" I really find a great resentment against you because of it. I am really still thinking about this— "Why did you do this to me?".

Ongka: Well, all right, I'll tell you. If I had put you into a school, then you would have turned into a humbug. I could have had you married to somebody, but, you know, sometimes women marry and then they leave their husband and they go from man to man. They tell lies and they give a lot of pain and sorrow to their father. I thought to myself that I would look after you with my own two hands and you would raise pigs and that if I gave you in marriage to a man, he would pay for you and would look after you in turn.

If I did not do this and I neglected you, you would become disobedient and you would run away and you would give trouble to me; that's what I thought. That is why I tied you down at home like this. If there had been a school nearby, I could have sent you to it but, you know, in the past the only school was far away at Hagen. We lived out in the bush far away from the school. I had no car. I thought that if I sent the boys to school, they might play and go around and they would come back bad. I thought that as you were a girl, if I sent you to school, some men would seduce you and they would take you away from me. The others would say, "Oh, look what the daughter of this man had done and where she is," and I would suffer pain from this, and therefore I thought I would keep you at home and from there I would give you in marriage to a man. Now people really know your reputation, and as a result of this I am well pleased with you and your husband is pleased with you as well. Everybody likes you very much because of all this work that you do.

AJS: Yara, what do you think of these remarks by Ongka on this matter?

Yara: Well, I do hear what he is saying. Yes, previously I did not really understand these things. Well, now I do have three children and I am tied to all the work I have had to do. I had to start doing this when I was a little girl and worked for my mother.

When I think that my children might have to do the same kind of thing for me as my mother did for her mother, and as I did for her, that really, to a small extent, makes me feel upset.

If only he had put me into a school and I had learned some good things, I could have traveled in airplanes, I could have traveled and eaten good food. I could have had a chance to have access to money and to use it more. If only I had gone to school, that is how I could have lived.

I am still angry about this, Christopher [Ongka's Christian name]. You have given me great heaviness about it, and I feel heavy also because of the death of my mother. I do really feel heavy about this because this is how my mother had to live when she was young and this is how I've had to live. You have made us both live this kind of life and I do feel angry about it.

AJS: Could you say something about how you have returned to your birthplace here.

Yara: Well, it has to do with my mother's death. You know, she wasn't really an old woman. Her youngest daughter was still in the early grades of school and her youngest son was not fully grown up when she died. And I wondered who would look after these two; there was no one at our back in order to support us. So I said to my husband, "Husband, you stay on your own ground, I'm going to go back to look after these two children. How can anyone look after their pig herds if I do not go? My father is an old man now. There is the home site of my mother and I must go there." And so I brought my own children back here too, and I looked after my younger siblings and the resting place of my mother also. That is what I intended to do when I came back here.

My husband comes and visits me here. There is nothing wrong about this arrangement. I look after the grave of my mother. I look after my old father and I look after my mother's place. I'm looking after my own children and my brothers and sisters. And if any of us die we will be buried in the same place here. If I die, David, my younger brother, can look after my grave. And that is why I'm living here and that is what I wanted to do when I came back here.

I feel happy because I'm looking after all of these people here. If I was to leave them and go to my husband's place, who would look after them? There is no one. Namba is permanently sick and I am happy to continue living here, and whichever of us dies here can be buried there also.

As for this matter that I am upset because he never sent me to school, that was some time ago and now I have three children of my own. My children are already big and I am myself on the way down in my life [getting old], but I am not really angry with him any more about this. It was just that, before, I thought that he could have sent me to school. But as he didn't, now that we are together here it doesn't matter, it's all right.

AJS: Your father was born even before the white men came to this area and he has seen a great many changes during his lifetime. What kind of life would you like your children to have in the future? Would you want them to stay here at home or would you want them to travel and live elsewhere?

Yara: If they should simply remain at home, I won't feel good about that. If they should have to do the work that I've had to do, I'd feel bad about that. You see, my father, though he had many many children, he didn't send any of them to school, just kept them here at home.

He just kept us here at home. His plan was to keep us daughters at home and give us in marriage to men. He was thinking about our own forms of wealth, like pigs and shells. That's why he kept us at home. He didn't send us to any kind of school. That was a mistake that he made. He just kept us here at home thinking the old thoughts about the old ways and not thinking about sending us to school.

As for my own children here, I don't want them to stay at home like this. I want them to go to school, even if it costs me a lot in terms of effort to pay the school fees. I want them to go to some good places and to be in school. In my mind, in my head, I really want them to go to school. I really don't want them to stay here at home. I really don't want them to live the kind of life I did.

AJS: What happens if, when they grow up, they get wild and leave you altogether?

Yara: With one part of my mind I think that if they do that, then I myself told them to go to school and if they leave me and go away, that's it then. I myself will just remain here at home. If they should happen to think of me, how I worked hard to send them to school to pay for the school fees, and now they are living a good life in a nice house and with good food and traveling around in cars, if they think about me because of all that I did for them and they come back to see me, then that will be just fine. On the other hand, if they go wild and do not come to see me, then that's all right too. I don't mind spending all my money. I really want to send them to school, and if they don't come back to see me, all right. However, if they do come back to see me because they understand all the pain and suffering I had as their mother that would be just fine. That's what I think about it.

AJS: Suppose you get old and there is nobody to look after you. What will you think then?

Yara: Yes, if I'm old and setting by the fire sick and they don't come back to see me, who will look after me? So, what if I am left to sit by the fireside while they are away in those fine places and maybe I'm losing my eyesight. I really want them to come and see me when I'm at that stage of life. I really am conscious that they ought to come back and see me.

If I don't see them, I shall be sitting here weeping at home. And how will I be able to write any letters to them to let them know that they should come back? I will be left here crying at home and waiting for them to come and visit me. I will be just sitting here waiting for them and saying, "These are my children, I gave birth to them, I want them to come back and see me." If they don't do it, what can I do? There is nothing I can do about it.

AJS: What do you, Ongka, think about all this?

Ongka: Right, let me talk about this. My daughter says that what I did was wrong but actually to some extent it was right. She herself is wrong in talking about it in this way. That is what I am thinking about it. Why do you think I held onto her so tightly and wanted her to stay at home? For this same reason that she now talks about, in case she grows old and dies and they just throw her corpse into a fire. She does not quite understand that if I had abandoned her and sent her somewhere else, then she might have been in serious difficulty at some time. And that is why I didn't abandon her or send her away. She said that I should have let her go, but I shook my head and said no to that, and now you see the whole point of it here.

Yara: Yes, that's all right. It's because of what he did that I'm here looking after him now, and if he dies I'll bury him.

Ongka: And she herself didn't understand that if she left here, in the end nobody would be around to look after her.

Yara: It is true that children really don't know what their mothers do for them. When they are just newly born, their fathers don't look after them. Little children stay in the hands of their mothers for a long time. Then a little bit later they recognize people and smile at them. Later their teeth grow. Later they begin to say "My mother," they say "My father," they ask for bits of food. Children really grow up in the hands of their mothers and they don't recognize this, and when we grow up we don't think of our mother and father. We run off and we find other people and turn them into our own, and that is something wrong that we do, it is something wrong.

If one of my children does remain at home, that one will look after me. Now if all of them leave here, will they come back to see me? Or will they not come back to see me? What will I do? There will be nothing I can do about it, nothing at all.

Ongka: Let me say something about this. I've been around in some of these outside places and I see what goes on in them. You know that when I was born, it was before white men came to our place. At that time people were obedient, but at this time, now that we have a government of our own, the children who were born in this later period really don't listen to their mothers and fathers. They really play around a lot. I have seen this matter thoroughly and I am quite alarmed by it. As for my own children, they did listen to what I said. The boys have grown up and married, the girls have got married to men and still they are obedient toward me. When I was a boy the government came, and then when I was a man in my middle age independence came. Now the children that are born after that time of independence are different.

There are young unmarried women, but suddenly you see they have children in their netbags. I ask what these children are, and they say these are children that are born outside of marriage! "What on earth is that?" I say. And as for men, I see they leave their parents and go and travel in other places and live around there. If someone says that the parent died, they say, "Oh, I see they died." They do not go to express their sorrow or grief by crying at the funeral. They just go away and leave their obligations behind. Men and women alike are just running wild, and I am very alarmed about this. And I think that when I was young I behaved myself properly. Now, since the white people came up, both they and our own people really aren't thinking properly. That is what I see with my eyes and what I think with my mind about it. Will they do things that are proper or will they not do so? That is what I wonder.

AJS: Yara, tell us a bit about how Ongka's sons do not take on his power.

Yara: Ongka did very strong things. God gave him a powerful mind. People say of those who go to school that some have really good brains. Ongka had really good brains for making moka exchanges, for marrying wives. He is better than everybody else. He makes strong speeches and good ones. He has had many sons, but none of them has taken over this power of his. If he dies, there will be no power in this place.

I would have got his power if only I would have been a man. I would have spoken as he speaks and done things as he does them, but God made me a woman. I could have succeeded to Ongka's brains, but because I was a woman I had to be married to a man.

If only I had been a man, I myself would have made the speeches. I would have spoken as he speaks. I would have done all the kinds of strong things that he has done throughout his career. But there it is, I was made a woman, and when I think of this and realize that at Ongka's death his power will be lost, it makes me very angry. I find myself very angry about this. Soon he will no longer do any of these things, and no one is taking over his power.

Both white people and local people know of Ongka. None of his sons has taken over his power and I as his daughter could have done that. I myself think, "Oh bother, if only I was a man, I would have taken over your power." In the place of the white people women do make speeches. There is the queen, for example. In our place here, among us brown-skinned people, women do not do that, women do not make speeches.

I know about how to do these things in my own mind, but these things just stay in my mind. How could I possibly get up as a woman and say that I am taking over the power of my father? Women just don't do this kind of thing. That's what I know, and I am very angry with his sons because his power will be lost and nothing can be done about it. He has connections both with the outsiders and the insiders. This is because of the strong brains that he had, and now when he dies all this will be lost. That's what I think, and I think if I had only been a man I could have taken over all of his power.

AJS: Tell us a bit about how younger people are different from the people before.

Yara: I'll tell you about my generation first. Our parents brought us up, and if we were daughters, they gave us clothing to wear in order that we would be able to attract a man in marriage and he would pay a bride-price for us. That was the kind of firm intention for us that they found. And we daughters had in our minds that we would go properly married in that way, bear children, get a bride-price. We didn't want our parents to become sick. We found proper thoughts and we wanted to live a proper life.

Now as for the generation of my children, they go around and try to find different sorts of husbands. They drink beer, they play cards, they have other foolish kinds of thoughts. They go and kill people and get into trouble. They do bad things. Some people spill each others' blood while drinking beer. They find uncontrolled ideas. We of my generation wanted to get married properly to men and to bear children for them and to make gardens and to rear pigs and to live properly in houses, and we wanted everything to be good for ourselves and our children. Now the present generation has lost touch with these thoughts. They do not think of rearing pigs. They don't of think how they can obtain money. They see themselves as bold in trying to steal things from other people. They covet what other people have and are strong in trying to get it. Women just think they can go and marry for nothing to good-looking men, and men just think they can take good-looking women for nothing. They do not really understand how their parents looked after them and brought them up. These are the kinds of thoughts they have, they are bad thoughts, they do bad things. New kinds of bad behavior keep on arriving and are being taken up. That is why people are not having a good life. That is why the place is not good. There is a lot of thieving. There are many rascals about who kill others. They are doing everything badly here.

AJS: Yara, when you were young, you decorated yourself and you danced in festivals. Now some of the churches say that people must not decorate any more. What do you think about that?

Yara: That was a different period, when there was a different law in our lives. The Lutheran and Catholic Churches had not arrived here and we were just on our own. At those times we did not understand things. None of us had been to school, and when we were young like this, our parents told us to decorate and dance, but now we listen to the Lutheran and Catholic Churches and we leave behind the old ways of decorating ourselves. That is what we do now that a different set of laws has come to us. I and my mother both did decorate before. They decorated me when I was a little girl. When I was small, Ongka found the things to decorate me that enabled me to dance.

Yara, 1995.

Yara with her three children, 1995, and Mande, a wife of Ongka, at Poklök, Kuk.

Yara tends to the grave, constructed in Catholic fashion, of her mother Rumbukl, 1995, at Poklök. Yara said: "We buried her in a fine place where she could look out over the Wahgi Valley."

AJS: Your father recently joined the Catholic Church. What did you think before, that he would one day join a church or that he never would?

Yara: I just wondered whether he would continue always in the same way, but later he himself decided that he would give all these things up and he would become baptized, and at that time he said he was giving up the old ways. He said that and he got baptized. It is because he felt he would die, and he did it in order to straighten out the road for his soul.

AJS: What do you think abut this suggestion some people are making that the world is going to end soon?

Yara: Yes, this talk is in the Bible according to the people who teach us about it. Now if only I was able to read the Bible, I would be able to say, "Yes, the world is going to end." But I am just here in my own way; there is nothing special about my situation. I don't know.

AJS: What about your two daughters? What will they do if the world comes to an end?

Yara: What will they do? I am feeling very sorry for them. They are so young. I mean, I'm grown up myself. If the world does come to an end, I at least have been taught about the church and will know that it had been foretold, but what about my two little children? They don't have any clear minds about this. Their brains aren't strong yet. How could they possibly know? If the world does come to an end, what on earth will these two do? And there's nothing I can do about it all.

Group Index

Epi-Kurup, 79, 97
Epilke, 80
Kawelka, xx, xxiii, xxvi, 1, 13, 44–50, 70,
    77, 93, 119, 126
Kawelka Kundmbo, 13, 45, 122
Kawelka Mandembo, 41, 126
Kawelka Membo, 41
Keme, 4
Kendipi, 54, 119
Kiklpukla, 75–7
Kimke, 14
Kitingambo, 3
Klamakae, 46, 79, 126
Kombukla, xxiv, 1, 44, 45, 77, 124, 125
Kope, 4, 88
Kukilika, 4
Kuli-Kele, 4
Kumndi, 95
Kumngaka, 97
Maplke, 3, 77, 79, 80
Minembi, xxiv, xxvi, 6–7, 13, 29, 45, 46, 67,
    70, 75, 119, 122
Minembi Andakelkam, 45, 121, 126
Minembi Engambo, 67
Minembi Kimbo, 91, 121
Minembi Mimke, 119
Minembi Nambakae, 6, 119
Minembi Papeke, 77, 122

Minembi Yelipi, 4, 91
Mokei, xxvii, 6, 7, 95, 112
Mongaepkae, 3
Ndika, 3, 26, 75
Nengka, 93, 123
Nggolke, 97
Nölka, 97
Oklmone, 3
Palke, 3, 26, 77, 79
Penambe, 4
Roklaka, 97
Romalke (Welyi), 79, 97
Römndi, 7, 75, 97
Rulke (Welyi), 97
Tipuka, xx, 5, 17, 29, 44, 71, 79, 124, 126
Tipuka Akelke, 97
Tipuka Eltimbo, 48
Tipuka Kendike, 4, 13, 44, 91, 97
Tipuka Kengeke, 4, 91, 124, 126
Tipuka Kitepi, xxi, xxiii, 4, 24, 28, 70, 93,
    105, 122, 126
Tipuka Ndikambo, 4, 46
Tipuka Oklembo, 4, 6, 26, 28, 46–7, 48–9,
    71, 105, 122, 126
Tipuka Wanyembo, 4, 28, 68, 97
Ukini, 77, 97
Waklpke, 97
Yamka, 4, 6–7

Proper Name Index

Anyan, xvii
Black, John, 8, 10, 112
Collins, J., 111
David (Ongka's son), xxv, 131
Edwards, Murray, 6, 112
Engk (Kaw. Klammbo), 26
Gibbes, R., 111
Gilliard, E.T., 64
Greathead, George, 7
Hallstrom, Sir Edward, 8
Hiatt, R, xx
Ik (Kaw. Membo), 44–5, 125
Ka (Tip. Oklembo), 26
Kae (Min. Papeke), 120
Kae (Ongka's wife), 28
Kaepa (Ongka's father), 1, 13, 26
Kakl (Kaw. Klammbo), 14, 16
Kalimb (Kaw. Kurupmbo), 46, 126
Kanamb (Min. Kimbo), 121
Kandekl (Kaw. Klammbo), 16
Karakl (Kaw. Klammbo), 38
Kaukla (Yamka), 7
Ken (Kaw. Membo), 110
Ken (Tip. Oklembo), 13, 56
Kerua (Nengka), 94
Kilwa (Kaw. Klammbo), 13, 47
Kimbit (Ongka's sister), 13
Klönt (Kaw. Membo), 46
Koepa (Kaw. Klammbo), 26
Kokl (Ongka's sister), 13, 14, 56
Kongrui (Tip. Oklembo), 46
Kont (Kaw. Membo), 10
Kot (Tip. Eltimbo), 56
Kowa (Tip. Kengeke), 125
Krae (Kaw. Mandembo), 126
Kuk (wife of Ndopaem), 6
Kuk (Minembi), 119
Kuma (Ongka's son), 89–90
Kuma (Tip. Oklembo), 56
Kur (Kaw. Membo), 1, 44, 125
Kuri (Tip. Kitepi), xxiii, 55, 69, 93, 95
Leahy brothers (Michael and Danny), 3, 111, 112
Lists of names, 47, 97
Mae (Kope), 88
Maep (Min. Nambakae), 6
Mair, L., 7
Makla (Kiklpukla), 75–7
Mande (Ongka's wife), 28, 55, 56
Marcus, G. and M. Fischer, xix
Mberem (Kaw. Kundmbo), 119
Mberem (policeman), 27–8, 112
Mel (Kaw. Klammbo), 38
Mel (Kaw. Kurupmbo), 124
Mel (Kumndi), 55, 95
Mel (Tip. Kendike), 13, 56
Mel (Tip Kitepi), 7
Mel (Tip. Oklembo), 13
Meng (Klamakae), 126

Mera (Kaw. Kurupmbo), 73, 120
Mit (Tip. Kendike), 55
Mitipa (Tip. Eltimbo), 26, 56
Mökö (Kaw Kundmbo), 126
Muli (policeman), 68
Namba (Ongka's son), xxi, xxv, 28, 30, 133
Ndakla (Tip. Kendike), 52
Ndamba, xx, 131
Ndau (Kaw.) 28
Ndekane (Kaw. Klammbo), 38, 45, 47
Ndekanga (Min. Papeke), 52
Ndoa (Kaw. Klammbo), 14
Ndoa (Kombukla), 45
Ndopaem (Min. Nambakae), 6
Nggaep (Tip. Kitepi), 69–70, 71
Niki (Kombukla), 124, 125
Nikint (Kawelka), 45
Nikint (Kaw. Klammbo), 26
Nikint (Kaw. Kurupmbo), 7
Nikint (Tip. Kitepi), 28
Nindi (Min. Papeke), 77
Nomane (Kaw. Membo), xxiii, 95
Nöni (old bachelor), 15–16
Nöni (Kaw. Klammbo), 13, 26
Nukint (Tip. Kitepi), 56
Ongka, *passim*; his assoc. with
    policemen, 27, 67;
    his assoc. with social anthropologist, 55,
        76, 127;
    meaning of his name, 1;
    his mother, 14;
    'Ongka's big moka' (film), 55, 60
Ongka (Tip. Kelmbo), 110
Oni (Kaw. Kurupmbo), 46, 126
Opa (Kaw. Membo), 110
Öi (Kawelka), 45
Öruma (Kaw. Klammbo), 13
Pakl (Min. Andakelkam), 121, 122
Palyim (Kaw. Kundmbo), xxiv
Pangk (Tip. Kengeke), 125
Parka (Minembi Yelipi), 6
Parua-Kuri (M.P.), xxiii, 55, 56, 91–2, 93–4,
    123
Pau (Ongka's wife), xviii, 6, 26, 56
Pena (Kaw. Klammbo), 13, 72, 73
Pera (Min. Yelipi), 56
Pik-Ruin (Kaw. Kundmbo), xxvii
Pokl (Kaw. Membo), 52
Prince Charles, xx
Pulti (Tip. Oklembo), 56
Pundukl (Kaw. Klammbo), 13, 26, 72, 73
Puri-Ruing (M.P.), xxvii
Raem (Ongka's daughter), 1, 26, 56
Raem (Ukini), 122
Rambe (Ongka's sister), 13, 14
Reuben-Parua (M.P.), xxiv, xxvii
Rokla (Tip. Oklembo), 29
Roklpa (Kaw. Klammbo), 45
Rona (Min. Engambo), 67

Rop (Tip. Kitepi), 7
Ross, Father W., 112
Rön (Tip. Oklembo), 28
Ru (Kaw. Kurupmbo), 119
Ruing (Nengka), 93
Ruk (Ongka's wife), 28
Rumba (Klamakae), 10
Rumba (Ukini), 95
Rumbukl (Ongka's wife), xxi, xxv, 28, 131
Ruri (Kaw. Kurupmbo), 89
Simpson, Colin, 8
Stewart, Pamela J., xvii, xviii
Strathern, A. J., 15, 44, 55, 76, 119
Strauss, Revd.H., xix, 112
Tape (Min. Papeke), 122
Taylor, J.L., 3–4, 6, 8
Tiki (Kaw. Klammbo), 13, 72, 73

Tikimb (Klamakae), 125
Tilaka (policeman), 68
Tip (Kaw. Klammbo), 16
Tischner, H., xix, 112
Ui (Tip. Oklembo), 28
Ukl (Kaw. Membo), 48
Vicedom, Revd.G., xix, 112
Wai (Tip. Kitepi), 55
Wamb (Mokei), 95
Watson, V., xvii
Weipö (Min. Andakelkam), 121
Wonom (Tip. Kitepi), xxiii, 126
Wora (Tip. Oklembo), 26, 56
Wöya (Nengka), 123
Yaklaka (Yamka), 6
Yara (Ongka's da.), xxv, xxx, ch.16 passim

Place Index

Angekl River, 125, 126
Angepina River, 121
Australia, 113
Baiyer Valley, 26
Canberra, 116
Chimbu, 27, 68, 112
Dei Council, 93, 111
Ekit Kuk, 122
Enga, 3, 113
England, 113, 116
Ep, xxi
Epamekui, 46
Gumants River, 88
Ialibu, 112
Jimi Valley, 3–4, 17, 26, 28, 37, 38, 46, 48,
    52, 54–5, 65, 68, 79–89, 126
Kaepa, 122
Kelua, 3, 6, 111
Kenankormanga, 46, 47
Kenanmanga, 45
Kiningangmul, 47
Kin Pup, 120
Kitip, 46, 54
Koklnge, 46
Komapana, 122
Konde, 45
Kopakana, 38, 46
Kora, 93, 121
Korn, 112
Kotna, 68
Krapna, 67
Kuk, xxi, xxvii, 14, 131
Kuta, 112
Kutubu, Lake, 11
Madang, 112
Mala, 112
Maninge, 123

Maplka, 112
Mbukl, xx, xxi, xxv, xxvi, 1, 4, 14, 48, 93,
    95, 112, 120, 123, 126, 131
Mendi, 11, 112
Miti Ku, 6
Mokla, 122
Morobe, 112
Mount Giluwe, 75
Mount Hagen; town, xvii, 36, 89, 112;
    mountain, 75
Muglpin River, 79
Möka River, 4, 16, 46, 65, 121, 126
Ngolke, xxiv
Nondugl, 8
Nunga, 70
Ogelbeng, 75, 111, 112
Okla, 45
Ombil River, 46, 65, 124
Ombin, 79
Pangia, 112
Penga (Pingapöngamb), 111
Pil River, 125
Pilpana, 46
Pintpint, 79
Pokalpana, 26
Poklök, xx, xxvi, 95, 131
Port Moresby, 13, 75, 76, 93, 113, 126
Raporong, 1
Reipamul, 112
Sydney, 116
Tairora, xvii
Tari, 112
Tiki, 75
Urunga, 127
Wabag, 112
Wahgi, 4
Weip, 6

Subject Index

"A Death to Pay For" (film), xxvii
adultery, 7, 29, 69
agency, xix
allies, 4, 42, 47, 49, 63, 65
anger, 51, 132
arrows, 49
axes, 3–4, 18, 38
barkcloth, 11
beer, xxiv, 94, 136
betel nut, 95, 103
big-men, xxvi, 13, 26, 45, 55, 56, 67, 121, 126
birds; See eagle, cassowaries, brush turkey, cockatoo, hornbill, birds of paradise; puklör, kondopakl, 82
birds of paradise; white (kurl), 55, 85; mek, 60, 76, 121; ribbon-tail, 64
bossboys, 7–8, 67, 91
brush turkey, 80
cargo ideas, 75, 113; See also money cult
cars, xxi, 29, 30, 95
cassowaries, 16, 45, 49, 52, 54, 56, 69, 82, 93, 126, 127
Catholic Church, xxv, 136, 139
cattle, 56
cemetery-places, xxv, 15, 16, 27, 61, 75
ceremonial grounds, 52, 95, 123
children; See games, parent-child relations
churches, xxvii, xxix, 136
cockatoo, 82
coffee, 111, 127
compensation, xxiii, xxviii, 7, 29, 41, 42, 49, 60, 65, 71, 73, 94
cooking, 12, 14–15, 21, 42, 63, 88
Councilors, Local Government, 10, 75, 92
cordyline, 44, 60, 91, 124
courting, 3–4, 17–18, 25, 119
courts, 69–70, 116, 127
dances; See under decorations
decorating oil, 11, 93, 113
decorations, at dances, 15, 42, 53, 76, 91, 123, 136
development, local, 132, 135
divination, 11, 57–8, 61, 70, 72, 126
divorce, 30
eagle, 52, 82, 121, 126
el nino, xxix
el pint pint, 63
elections, xxiii, xxvi, xxvii, 10
exhumation, 57, 67
firethong, 58
fish, 17, 52, 81–2
flute, 44
food, 17, 19, 72, 81, ch. 5 passim, ch. 12 passim; preservation of, 23; See also cooking, food plants
food collection, 17, 19, 23, 47; See also hunting

food plants, ch. 5 passim, 105; See also winged beans
frogs, 6, 16, 23
funerals, 27–8, 57, 60–2, 92, 110
gambling, 136
games, children's, 11–18, 19–20
gangs, xxviii
gardens, 17, 21, 26, 37, 65, 82
ginger, 23
ghosts, 11, 15, 22, 27, 43, 51, 58, 60, 61, 70, 75; See also sacrifice
God, 73, 135
gold, 112
guns, xxiv
Hagen show, 88
hornbill, 3, 85
horticulture; See gardens
hunting, 1, 16–17, 22–3, 80, 82
husband-wife relations, 26, 27, 28, 30, 36, 92
in-laws, 30, 36, 49, 132
Independence, 91, 93, 104, 116, 135
jail, 7, 8, 68
keka, 25
Kiaps (government officers), 6–10, 69, 123
Kina (P.N.G. currency), 55
kinship; brother-sister relations, 30, 79; affines, 30, 36, 56, 71; cousins, 47; pam, 56, 93, 94, 126, See also parent-child relations
koa mak pendant, 53
land, xxviii
lizard, 3, 87
luluai, tultul, 7, 67, 91
Lutheran Church, 136
lying, 75, 77
magic, 27, 52–3, 57, 60, 93
marriage, 25, 55, 69, 79, 88; bridewealth at, 3–4, 6, 18
See also husband-wife relations
marsupials, 12, 17, 22, 51, 81, 85, 86, 126
medical orderlies, 10
Melpa, xvii
Members of Parliament, xxvi
memory, xviii
men's house, 52, 57, 63
millennium, xxix
missions, 112
modernity, xix
moka exchange, xxiv, xxviii, xxix, 15, 28, 52–6 72, ch 13 passim
money, 55, 112, 123, 127, 132; money cult, ch 11 passim; money raising enterprises: See coffee, cattle, trade stores
murder, 30, 45, 70, 89, 126
netbags, 51, 103, 131
noman, xix
ocher, 52

old people, attitudes towards, 51–2; attitudes of towards young people, 94–5
origin stories, 79
paddle–spade, 37
paint, earth, 48, 52, 57
pandanus, 1, 11, 37–8, 51, 60, 87–8
parent-child relations, 1, 13–14, 17, 18, ch. 3 *passim*, 30, 36, 46, 51, 89, 125, ch. 16 *passim*
personhood, xix
pigs, 22, 26, 42, 63, 65, 92; naming of, 55, 95; *See also* cooking, wild pigs
pit-pit, 19–20, 22, 38, 63
plantations, 111–12, 116
plants; *kenggopa,* 22; *koepka,* 63; *koki,* 51; *kuklumb,* 52, 58, 63; *kundumb,* 57; *mara,* 17, 57, 60, 63; *mit,* 46; *mul tei* 17; *ndulkina,*17, 68; *neng,* 72; *pokan,* 63; *towakl,*52, 59; ginger, 23; *See also* food plants, cordyline
plumes, 54, 91, 120; *See also* decorations, hunting, trade
pokla mbo, 52
policemen, 27–8, 67–8, 71, 112
polygyny, xxviii, 69, 75, 77
punishments, 6, 12, 19, 68, 71, 73, 77
rape, 41–2, 45, 46, 48
refugees, 38, 46, 48
relational-individual, xviii, xix
revenge, 43, 57–62, 71, 73–4, 123, 126
ritual expert, 52–3, 57
road-building, 26
sacrifice, 12, 14, 16, 22, 27, 43, 51, 52, 57, 58, 65
salt, 11, 17, 69, 83, 113
school, 132
shame, 54, 61, 77

shell valuables, 3–4, 53, 59, 71–2, 73, 111, 112
shields, 49
sickness, 14, 16, 51
social change, xviii
songs, 6, ch 15 *passim*
sorcery (poison), 29, 43, 55, 57, 69–70, 72–3, 121, 124
speeches, 42–4, 47, 48, 61, 94, 97, 101–5
spirits, bush, 16, 112
spirit cults, xxix, 76
steel tools, 28
stone tools, 1, 4, 21, 38, 93, 113; transition to steel, 38; types, 4
surgery, 49–50
taboos, 81
theft, 15–16, 20, 65
time concepts, xix
trade, 6, 54, 111; *See also* shell valuables
trees; *kama,* 82; *kopil,* 82; *kopon,* 85; *kraep,* 27, 60; *menaplka,* 82; *mömin,* 85; *ui,* 60; wantep, 85; *wilaula,* 60; *wotil,* 85; more types of, 85; *See also* pandanus
tricks, 15–16, 38–9, 77
tultul, *See* luluai
University of Papua New Guinea, 127
uya nuts, 86–7
warfare, xxiii, xxiv, xxvi, 4, 6, 13, 29, 38, ch. 6 *passim,* ch. 9 *passim,* 126; *See also* refugees
white men, 3–10, 38, 54, 56, 77, 92; *See also* Kiaps, ch. 14 *passim*
wild pigs, 80, 86
winged beans, 88
witchcraft, 3, 74
women, and gender, ch. 16 *passim*
work, 21, 26, 36, 38–9, 92, 110, 131